Lessons Learned

in the School
of Hard Knocks

Charles E. Cravey

Published by

IN HIS STEPS PUBLISHING
6500 Clito Road
Statesboro, Georgia 30461 (USA)

All Scripture References are from the King James Version of
the Holy Bible (KJV) unless otherwise noted.

Printed in the United States of America
on Acid-free paper.

ISBN: 1-58535-220-9

Longfellow -

- Be still sad heart and cease repining;
Behind the clouds the sun is shining.
Thy fate is the common fate of all,
Into each life a little rain must fall,
Some days must be dark and dreary.

Dedication

To my dear and sweet grandchildren—

Meghan and Benjamin

Contents

INTRODUCTION:

I have learned most everything in life the "hard way." From early on I was the incorrigible kid, inquisitive, rambunctious, exploring the world around me with great interest in how things worked. As such, I would often encounter things without any warning. There were many near-misses along the way in which I could have so easily been electrocuted or annihilated by that inquisitiveness. Yet, as such, I've learned from those experiences a lot of hard lessons that most children never learn because of wise parents who teach them not to do or touch certain things.

I've heard about the *"School of Hard Knocks"* all of my life, and have chosen that as part of my subtitle, for I've been in that school and have learned a lot of practical principles. In the pages to follow, you will discover some of those "hard knocks" learned the hard way. Hopefully, what I share will be of important significance to you, the reader.

Dr. Charles E. Cravey
April 2011

Hard Knock U

Hard Rock U (University), reserved for those poor souls who have to learn lessons in life the hard way, is growing by leaps and bounds. Matriculation fees are very costly and are seldom paid in full. Some students never graduate, remaining in the classroom for life! Stubbornness, Hardheadedness and Ignorance are three of the most attended classes. To achieve the opposite of these three would lead a person to a degree and graduation. Life becomes easier and less stressful for the lucky graduate as he/she sets out on a new course in life, putting into practice the tough and hard lessons learned.

I've been in this University all of my fifty-nine years and have learned innumerable lessons, most of them learned the hard way. This book is a vain attempt to share those lessons with you, the reader, in the hope that they will alleviate your having to experience them first-hand. I've paid my tuition and dues in full so you won't have to. However, if you desire, the University is still taking students eager to learn life the hard way! Admittance is simple. You do not have to do anything, just remain where you are and refuse to accomplish anything in your life! Good luck.

GONE FISHIN'

Had it not been for my dearly departed oldest brother, Raymond, I would not be here today to write this article. He saved me from drowning one day at the Coca-Cola Pond near our home. That was our favorite fishing and swimming spot and was only a short mile's journey from where we lived. Fish were plentiful and easy to catch there with worms we would dig up from behind the outhouse. Most of the time we would return home with a string full of bream and bass caught with cane poles, but the most fun would be in swimming. One end of the pond was shallow enough for me to wade and attempt swimming in, but I never dared venturing further than the demarcation line we had set for I couldn't swim.

I remember that traumatic day when I slipped from the banks of the Coca-Cola Pond into its dark, murky waters. It had rained hard the previous day, and the banks were really slippery. I was fishing alone about 100 feet away from where Raymond was fishing. All of a sudden, I hung what I thought to be a large bass and did not have the strength to pull him in. I started shouting to Raymond to come help me, but he was preoccupied with catching a fish of his own. Wanting to impress him with my big catch, I struggled mightily with the beast on the other end of the line, only to give way to the mud on the bank. I slipped into the water without warning and began what seemed like an eternity of bobbing up and down and taking water into my lungs. The saying is true for I saw my life flash quickly before my eyes during the experience. I just knew I was going to die right then and there, but just in the nick of time, Raymond pulled me from the water, saving me from my impending fate! After a few minutes of heaving and spitting up water, I thanked Raymond for what he had done. I then walked the mile back home by myself vowing never to fish there again! Of course, within a week I was back at the pond fishing with some of my buddies!

There were many such experiences in my early years like the one mentioned above. There was the near-drowning at the railroad trestle creek at Little Ocmulgee State Park; the near-drowning at Horse Creek near Lumber City, Georgia; the near-drowning at the whirl-hole near Scotland, Georgia; and the near-drowning at the newly built swimming pool near the old South Georgia College building in McRae. A friend and I had climbed a fence around midnight and had taken a dip in the shallow end. It was hard to see anything, but we enjoyed the cool water on a hot, July night. I walked around to look at the deep end and slipped on the wet border and fell into the pool. My friend, Donnie Conner, pulled me from the jaws of death once again.

How ironic it is that my brother Raymond died saving two other persons during my first year at Seminary! It was at the whirl-hole, where Raymond had gone fishing after work on that Thursday evening. Near dark Raymond apparently heard the commotion of a mother and three-year-old daughter struggling in the water just below where he was fishing. Both had slipped into the whirling waters and were near death when Raymond reached them from the sand bar from which they had slipped. He had reached in and grabbed the child first and put her on the bank and had then pulled the mother to safety. While helping her reach the sand bar, he slipped into the whirl-hole and drowned! Again, it is ironic that my brother Raymond had saved several souls from drowning but could not save himself! You see, Raymond had never learned how to swim!

My brother Raymond will always be my biggest hero. His name will never appear on a list of national heroes, but it will always be listed in my heart and in the hearts of others whom he saved.

Today, I usually steer clear of any water, but did eventually learn enough about swimming to hopefully save myself or someone else from drowning. I'm just not that big of a fan of swimming and have learned to greatly respect the water, although my respect and lessons learned came from the School of Hard Knocks!

Bread of Life

You and I have an unrelenting desire and hunger for life. Whether it is a hunger for truth, love, knowledge, to belong, to express ourselves, for justice, hunger of the imagination or of the mind, or the hunger for significance, we are constantly seeking fulfillment. I must admit, however, that I have discovered that no one thing will meet all of these hungers. The only way to become full and content is to feed upon the "Bread of Life" found only through a relationship with Jesus Christ. He offers the only "Bread" of satisfaction and fulfillment. It is like oxygen to the body.

In Saint John's sixth chapter we learn of that "Bread" which can satisfy the human soul. In the beginning of that chapter, John records the amazing miracle of how Jesus fed the 5,000 people with 5 barley loaves and two fish received from a young lad. Jesus simply divided that which existed, and it multiplied when passed from person to person. There were actually twelve baskets left over from the distribution! Truly amazing works from an amazing God!

It is when we truly discover that God is the bread of life that we begin living the fruitful and meaningful existence He has designed for us. His Word *is* LIFE. He is the eternal water that will quench our thirst from which we will never thirst again (spiritually). Trust Him and believe in His ability to bring new life into your soul today and begin to experience fullness and contentment. A new life awaits you if you desire it to happen. God bless.

Things a Family Must Have

Families come in all different colors, compositions and demeanor. I found it odd the other day to search through the Want Ads in a large city newspaper to discover the following entries:

Women Seeking Men
Men Seeking Women
Men Seeking Men
Women Seeking Women
55+ Category - I guess they're looking for anything!

What strange categories we have today for people seeking to create "family." On one of the TV networks there is now a show with the title, "Women Who Like Men Who Like Men." What a strange combination that must be! Where has our "traditional" family gone? We have lost some very important things in this modern age which continues to threaten families everywhere. What are those things?

First, we seem to have lost our "roots." In order to survive as "family" we must know who we are and from where we have come. Who are your people? From what country/countries did your forebears come? Not only is it vital to know these things in our immediate family but also in our extended family. The old cliché is so true, "How can you know where you're going if you don't know from where you've come?"

Roots are important and are vital for tying us together with the larger family.

Next, there are "rituals" missing in a lot of families today. We must have stories of the past, of each of our forebears, a history of sorts that ties us together. Most youth today could care less about the past; they are only concerned about the present. Then, when they are older, they will regret not having done the research or asked the appropriate questions to discover their past. It is difficult for my family and my wife's family to even plan a Thanksgiving meal anymore. We are all so scattered that Thanksgiving has become a time of back and forth telephoning to decide what is going to be done. Then there is Christmas. Who's going to host it this year? What foods are we going to prepare? By the time that all has been confirmed, Christmas has lost its meaning!

Finally, there must be a religion to tie families together. It is important for us to share the stories of how we came to the faith, that which roots us in religion proper. What are you? Methodist, Baptist, Catholic? Are you aware of your first "religious" experience? Were you baptized? If so, when, where and by whom did your experience occur? These are things which will be very important to you and the family one day and will serve to keep the continuity in the family.

Let's begin to ask the tough questions about our family and to take more responsibilities for its future or we will be doomed in the next generation without knowledge of our past.

"Those who forget the past are doomed to repeat it."

Commitment

Psalms 37:5 states (RSV), *"Commit your way to the Lord; trust in him, and he will act."*

Most of us hate commitments, don't we? We find them very difficult and often long-term, if not forever, and we feel like we should keep our options open. Commitments tie us to some one or some thing. Today, sports heroes hold out to re-negotiate their contracts, regardless of the commitments made to their team. There is an ever-increasing divorce rate in America because people refuse to commit to their spouses. Millions of children go without adequate support because one or both parents refuse to commit to them. Our society used to be based upon TRUST, on a handshake, but now that has become virtually non-existent.

It is precisely to us that God speaks when He asks us to commit and trust our ways unto Him. The basis upon which our commitment is requested is God's commitment to us. His love is so great that He committed Himself to us by coming to Earth as a baby and later committing Himself to experience our pain and even that of a cross! His commitment to us brings LIFE and our trust brings Him joy.

Several years ago in Guyana, South America, our mission team had been working feverishly on a new church building for the folks in a small community. This community did not have running water or electricity. They survived merely on the basic fruits of the area, vegetables grown in each family plot, and animals they had raised from the wild. It was crude, but livable.

The church was finally completed and we had planned a service on our afternoon among the people of the village. A young man, Sekou, perhaps in his early twenties, had been watching our team all week with curiosity. He would often stop by and question us as to why we were building the church. I soon befriended him and he began working alongside of me, although he had never been to church before. On the afternoon of the service, we gave a very moving altar call and all of the team members went forward to kneel at the newly built altar. After prayers were uttered from the altar, we invited others in the congregation to come forward and to commit their lives to God's service as well. I noticed Sekou standing in the back door way of the church. I then witnessed his movement from side to side and eventually his slow, methodical walk to me at the altar. He hugged me so tightly and then asked if I would pray with him to accept the Lord. Sekou was saved that day and remains a very fruitful and faithful worker in that congregation.

Sekou's faith came by watching our team's commitment throughout the week to that little community and its people. He had never seen such faith before. Why, he wondered, would we take the risk and dangers of coming to his jungle to build a church? Today, Sekou knows why. Do you? Are you committed to Christ and are you serving Him faithfully? God is good - all the time!

We're Adopted

"Bless the Lord, O my soul: and all that is within me, bless his holy name. Bless the Lord, O my soul, and forget not all his benefits: Who forgiveth all thine iniquities; who healeth all thy diseases; Who redeemeth thy life from destruction; who crowneth thee with lovingkindness and tender mercies; Who satisfieth thy mouth with good things; so that thy youth is renewed like the eagle's." (Psalms 103:1-5)

One of my fellow United Methodist Ministers, Karl Stegall, once pastored that beautiful congregation at First United Methodist in Montgomery, Alabama. While there, Karl told the story of two little boys who had enrolled in the first grade and were asked for their birthdays by their teacher. The first little boy responded by saying he was born on January 1, 1984. The second little boy said, "I was born on April 4, 1984."

At that point, the teacher smiled and asked, "How can it be that you were born so close together?"

One of the boys spoke up and said that one of them was adopted!

The teacher knelt down before the boys and asked, "Which one of you is adopted?"

One boy spoke and said, "I asked my daddy one day, 'Which one of us is adopted?' and my dad knelt down and gave both of us a big hug and kiss and said, 'I can't remember anymore!'"

Isn't that a beautiful illustration? And is that not what Jesus was sharing in John 3:16 when He declared, *"For God so loved the world that He gave His only Son, that whoever believes in Him shall not perish but have eternal life"?* By saying yes to God's gift of love and accepting Christ as our Savior, God adopts us as His spiritual children. The Apostle Paul put it this way in Romans 8:17, *"Now, if we are God's children, then we are heirs, heirs of God and co-heirs with Christ."*

Once we are in the family, God accepts us as His own. He does not remember our past, our sins, our resentments or anger, our jealousy or envy. He embraces us as His children.

How thankful I am for a loving, heavenly Father who loves me, saves me, and adopts me because I have accepted His Son, Jesus, as my personal Savior. Have you accepted Christ as YOUR personal Savior? Have you allowed Him to work His miracle of forgiveness in your heart? If not, then I beg you to surrender to the Savior right now, without delay, and begin experiencing God's love and grace. Become a family member today!

Aaron and the Golden Calf

Exodus 32:24 - *"So they gave it me; then I cast it into the fire, and there came out this calf."*

The great Biblical character, Moses, has gone up to the mountaintop to hold communion with God alone while leaving Aaron, their priest, behind to keep the Israelites settled and focused. However, as soon as Moses ascends the mountain, the people begin to murmur and complain. They wanted other gods to claim as their own. Aaron yields to the overwhelming complaints and desires of his people. They brought to him their golden earrings and other priceless treasures and Aaron put them into the fire. Aaron's lame statement is so evident here, "And there came out this calf." A golden calf would not come out of the fire unless one was to take the gold and actually FORM the image of a calf from it!

At any rate, the Israelites are indulging themselves in idolatry and bowing down before this golden calf. Moses returns from the mountaintop and, after seeing their idolatry, becomes very indignant. He destroys the idol by burning it in the fire, grinding it up into powder, and strewing it upon the water from which the children of Israel were made to drink. He then turns to Aaron with anger to ascertain how all of this had come to fruition. Aaron's lame excuse was then regurgitated!

Aaron was frightened at what he had done. He was afraid of the act itself, and of what Moses would say. Like all timid men, he trembled before the storm which he, himself, had wrought. Aaron attempts to lay the blame on the furnace. "The fire did it," he declares. He will not face up to his sinfulness and shame.

As with Aaron, we are all ready to lay the blame for our sinful ways upon the furnace (life). Aaron basically tells Moses that he is a victim of circumstances, but Moses has better sense. We all cast our gold upon the furnaces of life hoping to receive a god in return that we can worship and bow before. When will we ever face the facts? No earnest soul can really lay its doubts upon a certain age or society lived in. A furnace can only fix and fasten what MAN puts into it. It cannot create a calf on its own.

The only hope for any of us is in a perfectly honest manliness to claim our sins. "I did it! I did it!" Let us refuse to listen for one moment to the voices around us which would make our sins less ours. It truly is the honest and most hopeful way to know ourselves and our God. When we have done that, then we are ready for the good news of Jesus Christ and all He wants to show us.

What is YOUR golden calf? What are YOU casting into the furnaces of life? To whom to you bow before?

Preacher on the Roof

Some years ago I challenged my congregation that if they would fill every available pew with worshippers on a given Sunday, I would go up on the roof and preach that morning's sermon. The congregants became very excited as everyone anticipated that Sunday. News reporters were there from various locations with camera crews and even Paul Harvey's reporter was on hand to witness the events of that day, particularly my preaching from the roof of the church.

Prior to that Sunday, my people were so excited and sure that the congregation would be packed, that some of the men actually constructed a temporary pulpit for me to stand upon while preaching up top! Of course, there were some skeptics and those who do not like to draw attention to such an event as this, but I proved my point that Sunday. We could all work much harder at bringing people to church with us and introducing them to the Savior. If it takes my preaching from the rooftop, then so be it! It was well worth the effort.

I became known as the "Rooftop Preacher" and went on to do it at two other churches in following pastorates, each time attracting a crowd and filling the pews. People were excited about such a venture and most gladly obliged.

Andrew is known in the Bible for one specific thing that

helped transform the world for Christ - he introduced his brother, Peter, to the Lord. As Catholics laud, Peter became the first Bishop of the church. At any rate, Christians recognize the tremendous faith and works of Peter in the establishment of the early church. It was to Peter, who earlier had denied knowing Jesus in the city streets of Jerusalem on the day of the Crucifixion, that Jesus said those piercing words in (scripture), "Thou art Peter, and upon this Rock I will build my church and the gates of hell shall not prevail against it."

What beautiful words said of a faithful and "changed" man! Would that Christ could depend upon each of us in the same fashion, when, in fact, HE DOES! We should be the church - its strength, its stamina, its instrument of grace.

One of my best friends, Donnie Conner, brought me to Jesus at the tender age of eighteen. That immediately transformed my life and direction and I have served the church since that time. I love those beautiful words from the hymn, "Since Jesus Came Into My Heart." Let me share a couple of its lines with you:

"What a wonderful change in my life has been wrought, since Jesus came into my heart."

"I have light in my soul for which long I had sought, since Jesus came into my heart."

That's what happened to me forty-one years ago and, to this date, I am happy and content in serving Christ with my entire being. What a WONDERFUL change!

I Will Always Love You

(a poem for Renee, my beloved!)

When the hands of time turn so quickly,
And our steps seem feeble and slow;
When the voices are faint and so distant,
And the faces we see, we don't know . . .
When the clouds of our future then beckon,
And our hands are then wrinkled and thin,
When the light in our eyes is much dimmer,
And our best years seem to have been . . .

I'll always love you,
With the last breath I breathe on my way.
I'll hold you each moment
And I'll treasure each day.
When we're both old and gray,
I will be there for you.
When time turns so quickly,
I will always love you!

For years we have lived in contentment,
Each moment a glow from the past.
Two children and then our grandchildren,
With plenty of love that will last.

Now moving from springtime to winter,
The cold comes from lingering years.
I'll be there to keep you so warm, dear,
And to brush aside every tear.

For I'll always love you,
With the last breath I breathe on my way.
I'll hold you each moment
And I'll treasure each day.
When we're both old and gray,
I will be there for you.
When time turns so quickly,
I will always love you!

Renee

For two months my dear friend, Donnie, and I prayed that God would send someone to me to help complete my life. I was invited one Sunday as a lay preacher to a little country Methodist church to share my witness since the pastor was on vacation. The pastor and I had a good relationship so he felt comfortable enough to allow me the opportunity of sharing my faith with his people.

When I arrived at the church during the Sunday School hour, there were approximately 15-16 people present. When Sunday School was over I was introduced to those present by a lay person who knew me. The Sunday School Superintendent, who was Renee's father, then approached me and said that service would begin in about five minutes and that I was to take the pulpit chair while the preliminaries were taken care of. He would introduce me and I would then preach, share, witness or whatever I felt led to do. Of course, I had brought my guitar to play and sing before I preached, and everyone seemed to be fine with that.

While sitting in that pulpit chair, I noticed a beautiful, small framed young girl sitting at the piano. She was playing the prelude for worship and then a song for the congregation to sing. I kept looking over at her off and on and hoped that she didn't feel as awkward as I.

I sang a couple of songs, shared my testimony, and then closed the service with prayer. I was to eat dinner with Donnie, his aunt and uncle, and a couple of other friends that day, so the first thing I mentioned to them was the young girl sitting at the piano and how nice it would be to get to know her better. They told me to call her up and ask her for a date that night for Donnie and I were to speak at a Baptist Church about fifty miles away in Collins, Georgia. I called and asked her and waited a good while as she asked her father if she could go. He answered affirmatively and I promised to pick her up around four o'clock that afternoon, along with Donnie and his girlfriend.

We had a great service that night, but on the way home we noticed that my mother's car was registering on empty, and we were about 25 miles away from the nearest station. We stopped on the side of the road and joined hands for prayer, asking God to get us safely to a service station. I held Renee's hands for the first time. We then continued our journey, forgetting about the gas situation, and found ourselves thirty minutes later pulling into a station 25 miles away!

We then stopped by Renee's little country church and we both went in to pray while leaving Donnie and his girlfriend in the car. Without turning on the sanctuary lights, we made our way to the altar to pray. There at the altar was the second time I held her hands. I prayed out loud, thanking God for giving us grace that night to make it to a service station and for bringing Renee into my life. I then asked Renee if she would like to pray and she did.

That was the beginning, and now, forty-two years later, we are still ministering to people across South Georgia and beyond. We have two children and two grandchildren who are all very precious to us and help to complete our lives together. Renee is only two years away from retiring as a teacher and looks forward to spending more time with the grandchildren. I'm still in the ministry but will retire in the next few years when I feel that it's time.

And to think that it all started with prayer, an earnest prayer each day with my good friend, that God would send someone to me who would complete my life! She continues to complete me and to bring happiness and joy to this old servant. *"Praise God from whom all blessings flow."*

Five Stages of Grief

Grief is real and eventual if we live long enough. Goodness knows I've had my share of it! I have lost a dear brother, a father and mother, uncles, aunts, cousins and numerous church members whom I've pastored for years. Grief is a natural and important process that actually aids in the healing of our sense of loss. Experiencing the death of a loved one is never easy. Grief hurts and takes time for full recovery.

There are various reactions associated with the grieving process that go from sadness to anger, numbness to pain and from guilt to fear. There are no clear cut processes or step-by-step directions for overcoming our grief because it is a completely individual experience.

I will be giving you some stages of grief here that I've learned from psychology classes, real-life experiences and others sharing particular characteristics of this grief process with me. We all react emotionally to grief in one way or another. Grieving the loss of a loved one is one of the most emotional and traumatic events we will ever experience, but there are healthy ways to face our grief and, over a period of time, to come to an acceptance of it and get on with the process of living. I do hope these following stages will help you through your periods of grief.

Psychiatrist Elizabeth Kubler-Ross was perhaps the first to define the stages of grief. Her stages actually addressed people coping with terminal illness, but they have become well-known in helping people who are facing grief. Here are the stages and progression they generally take to bring us to recovery.

I. Denial
2. Anger
3. Bargaining
4. Depression
5. Acceptance

Let's begin with Denial. When we have been shocked by the loss of a loved one, our first reaction is to deny that it has happened. We feel as though a mistake has been made that will soon be corrected. However, as time progresses and we realize that the death of our loved one is permanent, we move into the stage of Anger.

Anger can be very intense and people can respond to it in various ways through emotional outbursts, blaming others for what has happened or even holding resentment toward others. We can even express anger towards God for allowing this to happen. We can sense that God has acted unfairly towards us and then move into the next stage of trying to Bargain with God and others in our grief.

Bargaining is like a temporary truce with God, others and

ourselves. We will perhaps use the phrase "If Only" (i.e. "If only I had been a better person then mama would not have died!"). We attempt to bargain for life to return to the way it was, but it doesn't and so we move into a period of Depression.

Depression comes when the reality of what has happened really begins to sink in. When we realize that our loved one is not going to return, depression begins to take effect. It can surface in some as an intense sadness and withdrawal from others. We don't want to get out of bed in the mornings and we find it difficult to go through our loved one's belongings or to even take care of funeral arrangements. We begin to feel deserted and find it most difficult to carry on with life. This period can last for some time, but hopefully, we will move into the final stage of our grief, Acceptance.

When we have finally accepted the death of our loved one we are able to let go and to let God help us to move forward with our lives. Our grief lessens at this point and we begin the process of getting back to some form of normalcy. As the old saying states, "Time is the healer of all things." Remember that this process can take months and even years with some people, so allow time to be the healer. Give yourself space to move through the process and to grow.

May God bless you as you journey through the pain and suffering of losing a loved one, but may these stages bring some form of comfort and peace to you.

The "Timelessness" of God

Standing atop Stone Mountain near Atlanta, Georgia, recently, I could feel my spirit being renewed by the awesome and timeless beauty there. The mountain is thought to be over three-million years old and has remained virtually unchanged. From its peak one can see the city of Atlanta miles away. What a spectacular view! One wonders, while standing on top of the mountain, how God sees and could possibly care for these tiny little creatures down below!

As my spirit was being renewed, God led me to remember how discouraged I had oftentimes been while down in the valleys of despair. I realized then the prescription for my many moments of depression, anxiety and strife while in life's valleys. The prescription was that I should always remember the timeless and ever-present God Who created us and maintains our lives each day. We should also remember that He is always there, in control, and will see us through those valleys and bring us to the mountaintop again. He is both AGELESS and TIMELESS!

LORD, in my moments of despair, help me to realize your ever-present care. Heal me from my anxieties, depression and grief, and grant your gift of life to me this day. In Your Wonderful and timeless Name I pray. Amen.

"Go tell it on the mountain, over the hills and everywhere!"

POETRY PRAYERS

The following poetry prayers were written on a daily basis for the Warner Robins, Georgia, *Daily Sun* newspaper over a period of five years when I served the Northview United Methodist Church as pastor. The daily section was entitled, *Our Daily Bread*. Here are just a few of those poetry prayers for your use.

Out of my darkness, I cry out to Thee;
Heavenly Father, hear my earthly plea.
Fill me with hope and courage today,
And help me to follow in Your Holy Way! Amen.

Lord of the Universe, Father of all,
Guide, Lord, my footsteps that I may not fall.
Walk, Lord, beside me each step of the way;
And I will live for Thee, Lord, this very day! Amen.

God of my life, help me live today
In such a self-forgetful way.
Teach me to follow, to trust and obey -
And I will serve Thee, Lord, every day! Amen.

Speak to me, Father, with Thy comforting voice.
Help me to make Thee my one clear choice.
Humble my spirit, and Lord, let me be
Consecrated, Father, always to Thee! Amen.

Help us, O Lord, to seek and to find
That spirit of life; that Presence divine;
That cleansing stream of Calvary's flow.
Then, Father, we'll follow wherever You go. Amen.

Dear God, help us each day to plant seeds of love
That fall from Thy glorious Kingdom above.
Bountiful, gracious, and filled with such hope
That others therein, may find comfort to cope! Amen.

Our Lord and our Master, our Servant and King,
Help us, Thy Good News ever to sing.
Lead us to others who are lost on the Way,
And help us to show them Thy glorious Ways. Amen.

Recipe for Life

My wife and I thoroughly enjoy cooking together and using new recipes we've discovered. Through the years, we've learned how to use various spices to bring an old common dish to new life.

In similar fashion, we have found ways to add more zest and spice to our marriage, as well as to our individual lives. It takes so little effort, but many fail to try, usually ending in a stale and meaningless existence, as well as possible divorce. Americans have one of the highest divorce rates ever and the numbers are climbing daily.

We should always strive to add more spice to our lives whenever needed. We must seek out and find new ways and means, seek help from others, or just spend some quality time with one another to ascertain feelings and emotions. The results can be literally amazing.

Some years ago, Renee and I decided to celebrate "Date Night" on one particular night of each week with great success. We decided between us where we would go and what we would do. Be it a new movie at the theatre, trying out a new restaurant, or just spending quality time together without any outside interference -- transformed our marriage at the time.

Do not accept the mundane in your relationship to spouse, friend or life. Add some zest and spice to an otherwise meaningless existence and experience a transformed mind and heart. We did and it worked.

"Remember Lot's Wife"

Luke 17:32 is one of the shortest passages in the Bible. Three simple, yet complex, words are used by Jesus to symbolize an event in one person's life (Lot's wife) that had far reaching implications for time and eternity. *"Remember Lot's Wife"* speaks volumes to how we choose to live our lives. Choices pervade us daily: what to wear, how to live, how to treat others, chocolate or vanilla. We're not given a proper name for this woman Jesus mentions, but only an indication of her dilemma. Let me share the story with you as found originally in Genesis 19.

Lot's wife was rich in her faith and her husband was a very righteous man (II Peter 2:8). Lot's wife escaped from Sodom with him prior to the city being destroyed of all inhabitants. God had commanded them not to look back upon the city as they left, but Lot's wife did so and turned into a pillar of salt.
In the days of Abraham and Lot, few people were righteous enough to follow God and to have communion with Him, but these two had an enormous faith. You could say that Lot's wife was a favored woman in the sight of God. She was an example before other women in a day and age in which few were righteous. Abraham was her uncle by marriage and thus, she had every opportunity to know about and to worship God through this great servant and her husband. I guess you could say that she was "religious, but lost." Many fit into

this category today. They attend church regularly, pray in public whenever asked, serve on church committees or boards, but inside they are as lost as ever for they are not totally committed to serving the Lord. Lot's wife could not have helped seeing and hearing the angels who told Lot to flee with his family from Sodom, that wicked and perverse city. She knew the plan, but had become so entrenched with the people of Sodom that it cost her everything whenever, out of pity, she looked back against God's command.

Today, too many people are looking back to the ways of the past, sins they have committed, and are choosing that lifestyle instead of the committed lifestyle of serving Christ. The danger lurks around every bend for this person.

Jesus is speaking to the church in this scripture and reminds the congregants that the end is nearing. He desires their salvation if only they will turn to Him. If they continue to refuse His commands, they will become as Lot's wife, religious, but lost.

May this never be said about you, my friend. "Remember Lot's Wife" and be renewed in heart, soul and mind this day by the power of Jesus Christ.

Eloquent Speaking

"Though I speak with the tongues of men and of angels, and have not charity, I am become as sounding brass, or a tinkling cymbal." (I Corinthians 13:1)

I will never be accused of being an eloquent speaker. I strive diligently to put sentences together and to form a sensible phrase and do have a bit of difficulty in using the right words at times. *Ran* and *run* are two of my most abused words, among others. I always use them in the wrong tense and my friends, as well as my wife, are constantly correcting me. No doubt you will find some missed editing in this book where I've chosen the wrong word/s. Please forgive me for I was too busy daydreaming the week that we studied sentence structure and diagramming in high school English!

This beautiful scripture, I Corinthians 13:1, begins Paul's chapter on love/charity. His main intent is to let us know that we may have everything in life and be able to speak eloquently to the crowds and to God, but if we do not have love we are as loud and clanking as a brass instrument or a tinkling cymbal without a band. Love is the key element to life. He who is without love is most miserable indeed! Love is the opposite of hate, fear, depression, doubt, anger and a host of other negatives in life. Love brings consolation, peace, hope and a multitude of other attributes that lifts one's heart above the mundane. It is love for His people that nailed Jesus to the cross. It is sacrificial in nature and always giving, never taking. It is the act of doing for others instead of selfishly taking whatever we can. Love is LIFE!

I have seen parents go hungry in order to feed their children the last bit of food in their house. I have read about the untiring work of Mother Theresa in India in which she literally gave her life for those people as her sacrificial offering to God. Countless illustrations abound of people putting others before themselves because of love.

Do you truly love others? First, we are told, we must love ourselves and our relationship with God before we can love others. *Agape* love is sacrificial in nature and is the higher calling of Christ to any would-be believer. Do you have *Agape* love, my friend? Are you giving your best to the Master?

Righteous Affliction

Psalm 34:19 - *"Many are the afflictions of the righteous: but the Lord delivereth him out of them all."*

Afflictions seem more numerous among those who serve the Lord. It is one of the hazards of Christian service. Temptations abound. Ridicule comes often. The self-righteous are constantly seeking to bring the righteous down, and evil lurks at each turn in the road. It is a most difficult task for the Christian to remain focused on Christ and his service when such afflictions abound, but one **must** seek the higher calling, remain faithful at all times, and overcome evil with good.

In Matthew 26:41, we are warned that "the spirit indeed is willing, but the flesh is weak." In the very same verse we are admonished to *"Watch and pray, that ye enter not into temptation."* It is not a matter of "if" it comes, but "when" it comes, for surely it will.

Paul, one of the transforming and most powerful apostles of the early church, professed to having "a thorn in the flesh" with which he contended. In II Corinthians 12:7, Paul states that this "thorn" was a "messenger of Satan" sent to "buffet" him, to keep him humble and from seeking exaltation. In verse 8, we discover that Paul inquired three times of the Lord to remove the thorn from him and the Lord's reply came in verse 9: *"My grace is sufficient for thee: for my strength is made perfect in weakness."* It is then that Paul comes to an acceptance of his affliction by responding in the latter portion of verse 9, "Most gladly therefore will I rather glory in my infirmities, that the power of Christ may rest upon me."

Paul realizes and accepts his thorn of affliction. He decides that to "glory" in his "infirmities" would serve to strengthen him through "the power of Christ."

It is Paul, writing to the Ephesians at Ephesus, who states in Chapter six and verse 11 that the Christian should "put on the whole armour of God, that ye may be able to stand against the wiles of the devil." We should also be aware of these and arm ourselves with faith, truth, righteousness, and peace.

Other instructions include "praying always" (Ephesians 6:18) and watching with *"perseverance and supplication for all saints."*

Righteous afflictions WILL come. We should be prepared and ready to stand in faith on those occasions, armed with the power and strength of the Gospel of Christ.

Whatever Paul's "thorn" or "affliction" was is irrelevant. The focus should be on how God granted him the strength to overcome it by His grace and mercy. When we can turn our afflictions into blessings and see them in that light, then will they become "righteous" in the sight of God.

Danger Lurks!

Of all the countries I've visited, Costa Rica has to be my favorite. I've often thought of Paradise during my many trips there and how wonderful the people are, the beautiful surroundings, and of course, the most pristine natural settings in the world.

One of my favorite spots in Costa Rica is located in the northern zone near Arenal Volcano. This spectacular volcano is still very active and spews forth its fire and plume of smoke twenty-four/seven. It is fantastic to watch the fireworks at night from a distance and to hear the large explosions while huge boulders are throw upwards and then roll down the slopes of the mountain in a bed of hot, molten lava. On one side of Arenal are those refreshing hot springs that cascade down from the volcano forming pools of hot, stimulating water. Thousands of people visit this area each month and enjoy its near perfect weather. The hot springs is one of their major attractions.

In the midst of such beauty and awesome scenery lies the constant danger which lurks beneath the surface. In a moment's notice, the volcano could erupt and destroy thousands of lives in the process.

I'm reminded of the stories that locals in the city of Arenal shared with me on various occasions of the terrible morning in June of 1968 around 7:30 am when Arenal, after being dormant for over 400 years, erupted! On that morning, 87 lives were claimed by the volcano and three villages completely wiped out! As a result, three new craters now exist and are relatively active. People have moved a safe distance from Arenal since 1968 and are now more aware of what it can do.

Danger lurks with every Arenal and with our daily lives. We are in constant danger of the elements, but normally live our lives without thinking about the possibilities. To become overly concerned with the elements would be to render us paranoid. And then, without warning, it happens and our lives are forever devastated. What do we do or where do we turn, if we're lucky enough to survive?

I'm most thankful that I have the answer to that question. It was resolved many years ago at an altar in McRae, Georgia, when I gave everything I knew about myself to everything I knew about God to Him. At the tender age of eighteen, I surrendered, knowing then that I could not control the elements about me, but had heard of a Savior WHO could!

Are you living under the grace of God today? I pray that you are. If not, then surrender your life to Him today.

Harmony

I'm an avid gardener and love getting my hands soiled in the good earth and watching things grow. Our home is located in a country setting on a little over an acre of property. Tall pine trees are in abundance, and I have created several beds of azaleas throughout the yard. Camellias, lilies, pampas grass, crepe myrtle and a few other plants have been planted in a maze fashion, making it difficult for me to cut the grass, but I enjoy every single plant. My wife and I have also planted several young trees such as Live Oak, Poplar and River Birch. Thuja Green Giants (evergreens) line the back of our property and help create a wind break.

What a joy it is to see how both native and foreign plants thrive on our property in complete harmony with each other. In the spring they all come to life and spread their beauty and essence for all to see and smell. The varied colors produced in the yard create a postcard scene for others to pass and enjoy.

I've placed bluebird boxes around the property, and we have helped increase their population greatly with each box producing three clutches of babies each spring and summer. Hummingbirds also frequent our front porch where we hang colorful feeders. We love sitting there and watching them flit back and forth, enjoying the nectar we've provided.

Life abounds on God's Little Acre here at the Cravey home where you'll always find harmony. Everything thrives in God's perfect little garden, and so should we.

Heaven

At the age of fifty-nine, I've been thinking a bit lately of the future, especially since I have perhaps 15 to 25 more years left and am unsure as to how many of those years will still be productive. I haven't quite decided what I want to do in my next life (or even if I have a choice in the matter), for I can't seem to wrap my mind around the concept of just walking around heaven all day! Doesn't sound like a wonderful thing to me for I've been most active in these first years of my life. I'm not a good candidate for the slow, less-productive years of the aged. I literally loathe the day in which others will have to give care to me, be it family, nursing home attendants or others. But will we have a choice in the matter? Everything is uncertain concerning our future, so the best advice is to make the best use of these present years we've been given. Christians have always talked about heaven in terms of Paradise where we'll sing and dance and wile away the days by the "River of Life." The beauty of Paradise will overwhelm us, they suppose, but how long will it take us to become bored with such an existence?

Whatever your concept of heaven may be, it will vary from person-to-person. I tend to be more realistic and claim the Revelation of John approach in which John saw a "new heaven and new earth" in his vision of the future. I can easily wrap my faith around that concept--a new beginning on a new planet Earth in which we will be productive caretakers of God's new Kingdom and where everything co-exists in peace and harmony.

Genesis 21:1-5:

"And I (John) saw a new heaven and a new earth: for the first heaven and the first earth were passed away; and there was no more sea.

"And I John saw the holy city, new Jerusalem, coming down from God out of heaven, prepared as a bride adorned for her husband.

"And I heard a great voice out of heaven saying, Behold, the tabernacle of God is with men, and he will dwell with them, and they shall be his people, and God himself shall be with them, and be their God."

There you have it--a new heaven and a new earth. At some point in time, this earth will be destroyed by fire, purged and cleansed, and recreated for the next existence of mankind. Many have thought this purging fire could possibly be a nuclear holocaust or huge meteorite falling from space and crushing the earth. We can prophesy and attempt as many scenarios as there are people and still not arrive at a consensus of the future. Suffice it to say that one day there will be a new existence for us on a new earth. I can accept this concept far better than just floating around in the paradise existence of heaven all day!

Since we are all facing death and life beyond the grave, perhaps it's time each of us did a little more soul-searching and preparation for that major event.

I've just had a revelation that I may not make it through the next 15-25 years! What then? No need to worry for God alone knows the day and hour of my eventual passing. Live each day to its fullest: *carpe diem (seize the day)*.

Change

One of the great tragedies of life is waiting for things to change. Changes will come, regardless of who we are. I've recently been through thousands of dollars of tests by several physicians in an attempt to discover what is causing the pain in my legs and feet, as well as my shortness of breath. I feel like I'm beginning to fall apart, but I've been told repeatedly that this is "normal" for my age! None of us likes to hear that. We rebel against the predictions and state that we're just TOO young for these things to happen to us. Funny that my concept of what I look like changes every time I look in the mirror. That's not the same person! What happened to me?

Well, truth of the matter is that we are all getting older. Regardless of our level of vanity, we can do very little to stop it. None of the fad plans or programs out there on the market will really slow down this process. It's inevitable. We simply have to accept it and do the best with what we have at the moment. With our infirmities, we must press forward to do all that we can before we're unable to do them anymore.

In the waning years of my mother's life, I watched her failing health and heard her frustrations with being unable to do the things she once did. Her fingers became nimble and crooked with arthritis and could no longer hold a needle for sewing (her favorite skill). Her quilting days were now over and she was eventually placed in a local nursing home. Her health quickly left her, while there, and she only survived about three months. It really hurt to see mama in such bad shape and to know that those feeble hands once held me as a babe and nursed me to sleep each night.

Change will come, beloved. Are you prepared for it? Are you ready? Do not wait until it's too late. Enjoy life to its fullest today but also make preparations for tomorrow. God bless.

Early Morning Inspiration

Another early morning, 4:30 am, and I can't sleep. I stare at the alarm clock on my nightstand which hasn't had a chance to alarm for several mornings. I'm not tired, nor depressed, nor have symptoms of insomnia. My fifty-nine year old body just doesn't seem to need the rest of previous years. I remember earlier years when I could sleep until lunch on Saturdays. I guess now there seems to be so many things filling my mind - responsibilities, growing older, job security, grandparenting - that my mind awakens me rather than my body. Mama was right - with age comes more responsibilities.

I'm writing this at 4:45 am while watching an old movie from the 1960s. I occasionally glance at the movie while concentrating more on this article. It is important for me to get this right, for there will be those who come after me who will read this for introspection.

Inside, I'm still that young fifteen-year old pilgrim-- inquisitive, rambunctious, always exploring the world around me. I wanted to be a doctor and heal the sick. I wanted to be a missionary and save the world. I wanted to be a teacher who would instill words of wisdom into the minds of young people. I wanted to be a scientist and invent a cure for cancer. Instead, I became a writer, a poet, a preacher, and singer. I do not infer that these gifts are of lesser importance, but that dreams, desires and directions change as we mature into what God is calling us to be. I am now an intricate and complex part of God's overall scheme of things. Of that, I should be most thankful.

As I watch the movie's credits rolling past on the screen of my TV, I slowly lean back in my recliner and zip . . . I'm gone, fast asleep. My wife wakes me a couple of hours later and we're both off to take on the world again. I feel refreshed now after my morning inspiration.

Finding Your Way Back in the Dark

In the 1961 movie, "The Misfits," Marilyn Monroe asks Clark Gable a very searching question: "How do you find your way back in the dark?" Gable replies, "Just head for that big star straight on. The highway is under it. It'll take us right home."

Gable's point is clear. When we are lost, confused, disillusioned or searching for our way, there must be a clear focal point, a constant, a familiar sign that we can follow which will lead us home again.

There are those unchangeable things in life which serve in giving our lives direction. One of the most important is our faith. Our belief and trust in a system, an organization, or a being is crucial to finding our way. Without faith, we wander aimlessly, struggling for survival. We need a constant to hitch our faith to, a belief in something or someone that is far greater than ourselves.

When my wife and I were preparing for the birth of our first child, we attended Lamaze classes for prepared childbirth. Each week we were told to concentrate on a focal point while we did the breathing exercises and went through each step of labor and delivery. I remember it helping us tremendously during the process.

What are you focusing on? What is that unchangeable thing in your life that you have put your entire trust and faith in? Will it sustain you and give you life? I trust that your constant is Jesus. He will not lead you astray and always has your best interests in mind.

Lady

She came into our lives in late fall and claimed our home as her own. She had no collar of identification so we assumed she had been thrown out near our country home. She was a black and white Border Collie and just as friendly as could be. After a few days we began leaving food in a pan outside our front door for her and gave her the simple name of "Lady."

Lady began guarding our acre of property as her own, chasing away every stray dog that tried to enter. Most every night was spent sleeping on a matt at our front door. She greeted us each morning with her tale wagging and making small, grunting sounds.

Lo and behold, on Thanksgiving Day, Lady crawled underneath my pickup truck and dug out a hole large enough for her to sleep in. She pushed pine straw up around her bed to break the cold winds from getting to her.

The following morning I went out to the truck to feed Lady and bent down to look underneath. There, to my surprise and amazement, was our newly adopted Lady with EIGHT little black and white puppies! The Cravey family had just increased by eight little unexpected members!

Needing my truck, my wife and I had to help Lady move her puppies to a safer and warmer location, so we gathered up all the puppies and moved them to a bed we had prepared for them in our utility shed. We had taken our grandson's plastic swimming pool and put some blankets in it for Lady and her family. She took to it immediately and seemed to thank us with her gestures. There she and her puppies would be safe and protected from the freezing temperatures we were experiencing.

Lady's dilemma reminded me of that beautiful Biblical story of Mary and the baby Jesus and how she could not find a place to birth the Son of God other than in a hay manger in a cattle barn. In nature, God seems to provide for His own. We may not like the amenities but they always seem to suffice. Trust in God and He will provide.

Fascination

I've just returned from my first cruise which lasted five days. I was a passenger on the Carnival ship "Fascination" and was completely fascinated by the experience!

We left port in Jacksonville, Florida, and headed towards Key West and then to Nassau in the Bahamas. I had been to Nassau on several previous occasions while on mission trips, but this would be my first trip to Key West, Florida. I was not impressed with either port of call, but the ship was a different story. I met and talked with so many people that my head was spinning long after the trip.

There were over 2,000 passengers and 700 workers on board. The length of the ship was over three football fields and was a twelve-story structure with swimming pools, hot tubs, two large dining rooms, an art gallery, several bars, two large show theaters, a library, full service spa, and an entire floor dedicated to children and youth activities. There was putt-putt golf and also a jogging track. Our rooms were cleaned "twice" each day! The staff waited on and pampered the passengers around the clock. They were simply amazing.

I met workers from Romania, Serbia, Russia, Costa Rica, England, Indonesia, Africa, the Philippines, Panama and a host of other nations - 56 in all! They sign up to work an eight month contract with the cruise line and then have two months leave before starting back on a new eight month contract. I talked with a worker from Indonesia who shared his story with me. He is married with two children and makes $1,000 each month. His room and board are provided free by the cruise line and he is happy with the arrangements. He stated that most of his friends back in Indonesia make only about $3,000 for an entire year of work, so his job on the ship was very lucrative.

There are very few Americans working on Carnival ships, due mainly to the low salaries. The ones who do work are in higher positions such as Ship's Captain or another commanding post. All of the workers were extremely polite and cordial and made my trip very pleasant.

It was all smooth sailing until we headed into a very strong head wind on the way back to Jacksonville. The ship would list from side-to-side, making it a bit difficult to walk on deck, so I utilized the time on my bed putting these thoughts together for you.

What a "fascinating" adventure on the "Fascination." The food was great, the entertainment superb, and the crew was exceptional. Now my task is to convince my wife to go with me next spring. Wish me luck for she gets seasick taking a shower!

"O, Christmas Tree"

My wife adamantly puts up our Christmas tree the day after Thanksgiving each year. As if Thanksgiving wasn't hectic enough, I have no break at all until January 2nd. I really enjoy quiet, peaceful times more than the busyness of holidays. In my heart, I celebrate Thanksgiving and Christmas throughout the year, while many seem to need a designated holiday in order to celebrate. I guess that's what makes us all different.

So I humor my wife, children and grandchildren on all the special holidays of the year and take the celebrations in stride. To see the glow in the eyes of Meghan and Benjamin (our grandchildren) makes it all worthwhile. And again, there are always football playoffs and college bowl games that Thanksgiving and Christmas bring.

It is now the day after Christmas and the tree HAS to come down. It is quickly packed away in its storage box and put into the attic until next year. Again, it is tradition with my wife. She has to have her house in order again as soon as possible.

Isn't it strange that some people also treat the Christ in similar fashion by mentally boxing Him up and putting Him away until next Christmas! Perhaps our lives are simply too busy for Christmas after all. Maybe we're missing the true reason for the season. Could it be that we have left the real CHRIST out of our CHRISTmas?

Overdue Books and Life

I recently heard about a ninety-year-old man who returned an overdue library book after keeping it for 70 years! The fine on the book was over $3,000! Wow! Can you not imagine the guilt, grief and anguish that guy went through during those years? He had been harboring that guilt for way too long! It had to be taxing on him mentally and spiritually.

Many of us are harboring ill-feelings, guilt, grief and anguish in our hearts today. They serve no worthwhile purpose other than keeping us from experiencing the fuller life. Why do we hold onto the very things that make our lives miserable? When will we learn to let them go, pay our debts for the past, and begin anew?

I remember as a child harboring several books which I had taken from the elementary school library in a closet at home. They had been taken over a six month period and I actually thought that I was going to be able to keep them and no one would ever discover them missing! The mind-set of a nine-year-old boy is not very sharp and certainly wasn't with me. I loved books and wanted to be surrounded by them.

Well, to make this story short, my secret was discovered one day while my mother was cleaning out the closet. She wanted to know where those books came from. I attempted to lie about it, but I was never a good liar! She saw right through me and made me carry those books back to the school library the next morning. Mama went with me to see what the monetary damage was going to be (dues). I was embarrassed when confronting the librarian. She stared a hole right through my soul and I cringed. Mama asked her how much we owed in past dues. She was told that it would be $14.75! This was in 1961 and that was a lot of money to our family. We worked out a deal in which I would come to the library each day for the next two months and work for the librarian to cover that amount. I would reshelf books to their proper locations, take out the trash, sweep the floor, and do other minor little jobs for her.

I learned my lessons on past due accounts very quickly! It's a shame that many of us never have to face the music until our grief has consumed us. Are you harboring grief from the past? Are you past due in the account of your life? Pay up today and be freed from that anxiety and fear. Do not wait until just before the undertaker comes for your body to make amends. Do it TODAY!

The Human Touch

My friend, Terry, shared a story with me about an elderly lady who lived alone and would go down to the corner store each day and buy some small item just so she could feel the warmth and touch of another person's hand when she paid for it at the checkout counter.

Stories abound of premature babies in incubators who seem to thrive and survive through the touch of nurses, mothers and attendants. It is the gift of touch that can transform our lives, change our attitudes, caress our hearts, and restore us.

I remember the warm, fuzzy feeling I received at the tender age of eight when a beautiful neighborhood girl took my hand one day while we were walking home from school. She held it for almost a mile and we would swing our arms back and forth while walking. Her simple touch, be it childish perhaps, led me to fall in love with my first girlfriend. The only problem was that she did not see it that way! When I told her that I loved her the next day, the hand-holding stopped immediately! How quickly things can change.

Touch is an amazing thing. It can make a strong man weak, cause a small premature baby to grow, or give an elderly lady a reason for living one more day.

Have you touched someone near and dear to you today? Why not reach out and see the difference it can make in another person's life? You will be a far greater person for having done so.

Love is More Than a Casual Thing

I've just completed writing a new country song to be demoed soon in Nashville, Tennessee. Let me share with you the first verse:

"She wakes at five each morning with star-dust in her eyes,
While the babies sleep and I'm still dreaming dreams.
She cooks our breakfast, cleans the floors, and washes a load of clothes.
She's done this for a lifetime or so it seems.
She's a little bit of angel in a five-foot two-inch frame,
And for her **Love is more than just a casual thing!**"

I was thinking of my wife, Renee, while writing this one. I recall how she used to go through each of the things in her daily routine for us when the children were young. She would rise long before we did and do a myriad of chores prior to going to work for the day. She did this because she loved us and that love was certainly more than just a casual thing. It consumed her and gave her life complete meaning.

Is there someone in your life who is perhaps working over-time for you? Is that someone making the supreme sacrifice for your well-being and happiness? Why not thank him/her today, give him/her a big hug, and let him/her know that his or her love is greatly appreciated. You'll be glad you did!

Mental Plaque

My wife, Renee, just had a heart catherization due to a perceived blockage on the frontal part of her heart. Her cardiologist felt it necessary to go inside with the scope to see exactly where the problem area was. Luckily, there was only minor plaque and she would be treated with medication and exercise. This was tremendous news for us because Renee's father died of a massive heart attack at a fairly early age.

Isn't it amazing that technology can look today inside our hearts and potentially correct any life-threatening abnormalities! Would that we could so easily do this with the "proverbial" heart of man. Yet, millions of dollars are spent each year on counseling sessions and treatment facilities in attempts to discover our inner problems. Cures for such mental abnormalities are usually very complicated and uncertain in their outcome. Mentally, most of us carry enough plaque that, if left untreated or unresolved, will eventually destroy us. The human mind can only take so much mental distress. We are in need of a very experienced counselor or Savior.

The Bible reminds us that sin is overwhelmingly the culprit. Romans 6:23 states that "the wages of sin is death; but the gift of God is eternal life through Jesus Christ, our Lord." Sin, if left unresolved or unforgiven, is like a cancer that begins small and slowly takes life from us. Jesus came to earth and died for the sins of mankind but we have to seek His forgiveness in order to receive it and begin a new life. He's as close to us as our next breath. Call on Him today and find LIFE!

Leaving a Legacy

My friends, Terry and Patsy Deloach, have a three acre plot of blueberries near Brooklet, Georgia. Each year they give those succulent berries away to family and friends to enjoy. Renee and I will freeze several quart bags and share them throughout the year as gifts for other friends and family members, as well as for making delicious blueberry muffins, blueberry cobblers and an occasional blueberry cake. My mouth waters, even now, when I think about those wonderful, healthy and sweet berries!

I feel as though I've somehow helped perpetuate the berries by working with Terry each year to prune the bushes and to keep the grass cut between the rows. It has been well worth the effort and a labor of love for me.

Here's the catch: Terry, Patsy, nor I ever planted one single blueberry bush! We simply tend them each year. It was Patsy's father who had the dream, vision and land who decided one day to plant those acres with blueberries. They have now been a blessing to many others. Mr. Raymond Poss died a few years ago, but his dream and vision lives on as we celebrate the harvest each summer. We enjoy the bounty of his hard work and efforts, as do many others.

In life and death our lives and efforts should be to do something worthwhile for others; to leave a legacy behind that will bless people long after we're gone.

I've just eaten another one of Renee's cream cheese blueberry muffins and celebrated again the "life" of Raymond Poss!

True and Loyal Friends

Back in the mid-1970s, Renee and I were living in Fitzgerald, Georgia, where I served as pastor of Saint Peter's United Methodist Church. Renee worked at the National Bank of Fitzgerald where she met and became best friends with Diane Tucker, another bank employee. They have remained best friends now for the past thirty-five plus years and are constantly calling, texting and traveling to spend weekends together every now and then. Both now work in school systems in different locations and are able to schedule things around the same calendar. If one or a family member has surgery or a major event (marriage, childbirth, etc.), the other will do everything possible to be there. I think, at times, that they would even die for each other to save the others' life! Now that's "true" friendship and not just one based on a whim or passing fancy! True best friends are always there for you.

Diane has just called Renee to share Christmas wishes and the events of the grandchildren on Christmas morning. Renee's voice becomes jovial and immediately excited whenever she hears Diane's voice on the other end of the line. Their friendship is inseparable, strong. and ever-lasting.

Do you have a true best friend to invest a portion of your life with? Is there someone you can count on to be there whenever needed? I thank God daily for Diane's faithfulness to Renee and our family. She is a true God-send!

When It Snows

It snowed today in South Georgia, a very rare occasion, but one which evoked memories of past events in my life. I looked outside and saw the beautiful white, pristine countryside and remembered a traumatic event when, at age thirteen, a snow and ice storm enveloped our small part of the world. Everything was frozen solid for three days. We had no electricity and stayed barely warm, wrapped in blankets and sitting around an old pot-bellied stove. Our old wood framed home had cracks in the floor and walls and we could hear the wind as it whistled through. Our food supply became desperately low, so we began rationing what remained. I remember huge tree limbs breaking off and making loud thumping sounds as they crashed to the ground outside of our home. Everything outside was solid white.

Around 2 am of the second night of the storm, my brother Raymond and I heard a car slowly making its way up the old dirt lane to our home. We looked out the window from the foot of our bed and watched the headlights slowly creeping closer. It finally stopped for a brief spell in front of the house, a door opened, and we saw a figure being pushed from the vehicle onto the frozen tundra. The car then sped away, leaving the lone figure there on the road.

Our dad had been gone for two days on another binge, so we

immediately assumed that the figure on the road was him, lying there in a drunken stupor. Mama asked Raymond and me to go out and try to bring him in.

When we reached his body, dressed only in our Long-John underwear, we noticed that he was bloody all over. We tried to pick him up but eventually dragged him into the house. Under the pale light of our kerosene lamp, mama saw where he had been stabbed several times with a knife and had been bleeding. The cold had apparently stopped the bleeding. Dad was unresponsive and only made small, grunting sounds. Mama then sent Raymond and me down the lane to try and find a neighbor with a car to help us carry Dad to the local hospital, a couple of miles away. I went in one direction and Raymond went the other.

I knocked on several doors but no one would answer until I finally made it to our city policeman's house several blocks away. Time was of the essence because we just knew that Dad was dying from his wounds. The policeman cranked his old Chevy and told my brother and me to get in. We were still in our underwear and never once realized how cold it was. We only thought about Dad and prayed he would make it.

When we reached home again, the policeman came in and helped us carry Dad to his car, placing him in the back seat. Mama had taken off his old clothes and had dressed him in some warm, clean ones. She told my brother and me to stay at home until we had heard something from her as she accompanied the policeman to our local hospital with dad. Blood was everywhere in the house, and we just knew that Dad was not going to make it.

Without a telephone, we had no way of finding out how Dad was until late that next afternoon. The policeman came by to tell us that the local hospital had refused to take Dad because we had no health insurance. So Dad, being a veteran of WWII, had to be transported in the patrol car thirty-five miles away on frozen roads to the nearest Veteran's hospital. The policeman told us that Dad had been stabbed in several places and one had been near fatal, only a couple of inches from his heart! He told us that it would be a trying time for Dad over the next few days and that Mama had sent word back to us to stay put until she came home. Raymond was nineteen and could easily take care of me.

Raymond and I rationed out some saltine crackers and Vienna sausages until the ice melted from the trees and roads, allowing us to walk to town and charge some groceries at Fowler's store.

Two days after the ice melted, Mama came home from the hospital in the policeman's transport. It would be several weeks before Dad came home, so we survived as best we could. Mama applied for food stamps and we walked to town to receive the government commodities, bringing the food home in paper sacks. It would be enough to cover our hunger for the time being until Dad could return home and to work. We survived.

Thanks to the kindness of that caring policeman, Albert Browning, Dad survived and soon returned to work. Things finally settled down and we resumed our less than mundane lifestyle.

Later on, we discovered that Dad had been off with two brothers drinking on that near fatal night and had gotten into a fight with one of them. Both then jumped my dad, stabbing him several times and actually thought they had killed him! The V.A. doctors told us that the ice and extreme cold was probably the only thing that saved Dad. How ironic! The very storm that nearly took Dad's life was actually the reason behind his survival!

We all have storms which often seem fatal, but which usually serve to make us stronger and more determined survivors. We can pray they never come, but eventually they will. I've had several storms since that early one and each has served to make me a stronger individual. Still, I pray for the calm.

Sacred Cows

All of us have "sacred cows" which we protect, defend and honor. These cows can be both positive and negative in nature, so one has to be extremely careful when seeking to impose them upon others.

Let me list a few types of sacred cows and seek to give an explanation for their implications in our lives.

Unwritten Cows - A bureaucratic person would be a good example of this one. There are "unwritten" laws that govern how one lives, but one cannot point to a source of their origin. However, this person will defend those laws to the ultimate degree.

Written Cows - I'm immediately drawn to my years of service as a pastor to explain this sacred cow. Let's think about the bylaws and policies of a local church. These are often defended by the church and the pastor, and if someone steps out of alignment with them, the members have written laws to judge them by. A note of caution here--simply because a written law or policy exists does not necessarily make it right in all situations. Never seek to change one of these laws on your own for you'll encounter a barrage of conflict.

We need laws and policies in a civil society, but if we are

inflexible and insensitive to individuals because of those laws and policies, we begin to utilize them as sacred cows.

Turf Cows - These cows pit "US" against "THEM." A good example would be Republicans and Democrats. Never give in to the other side for that would expose a weakness that could be exploited. Our country is the way it is today because one side will do everything within its power to protect its point of view.

Denominational Cows - The Catholic Church, The United Methodist Church, The Southern Baptist Church, Jehovah Witnesses . . . . These and many others have their own theology and doctrines they swear by and live with. They are always pitting "their" modes and belief systems against all others. It is what makes them distinct and different. Never get into an argument or debate with them over one of their sacred cows, for they will defend them to the death!

Finally, there are **Personal Cows**. As with each of the other cows mentioned in this article, we have our own little set of rules and laws, often to our own detriment. These can become huge obstacles against freeing ourselves from the ties which bind. We fear change or anything which threatens "our" way of life.

Examine your cows today and ask yourself whether or not they are keeping you from completeness and wholeness. Your life and well-being depends upon it.

Sometimes Justice Prevails

It's December 30, 2010, as I write this, and I've just watched on TV another college bowl game featuring North Carolina and Tennessee. The game had no national implications, as far as standings are concerned, but did serve a lesson in how justice sometimes prevails, in spite of bad calls by the officials.

The player who scored what would have been the winning touchdown run by Carolina saluted the crowd and was penalized for doing so. The penalty brought the ball back to the original spot with a fifteen yard penalty tacked on for "excessive celebration." When did a simple salute to the crowd merit a penalty? God forbid our U.S. soldiers being penalized for such a salute!

Our society has become so sensitized to every little gesture by someone else that our courts are overwhelmed and the A.C.L.U. (American Civil Liberties Union) has a field day with their lawsuits. A simple touch can now be considered as sexual harassment. A well-meaning neighbor reaches out to help the person living next door and later discovers that the person had taken a bad fall in the yard and is now suing the helpful neighbor for leaving a pile of leaves for her to trip over!

When will we see such sensitivities for what they really are and reverse the direction we're headed?

Good news! Carolina finally won the game in the second overtime period by a field goal--no thanks to the referee who made such a terrible call for a young man's salute! Justice prevailed once again, and I was thankful. Good luck out there for it's a crazy world today!

In Loving Memory of Corporal G.T. Gray

by Dr. Charles E. Cravey

In the cold, hard belly of an Army tank,
Corporal Gray slept and never pulled rank.
A true, blue American from head to toe,
He soon became every Nazi's woe!

"Goat" he was called in high school ball,
As he played on that championship team;
Tough as nails and he never failed
To follow his destiny's dream.

Deep in his heart he was torn apart
By the men in the war he had killed.
But peace came to him in these latter days dimmed,
When he realized God's Holy Will.

Betty, his mate, stood with patient wait
Through these last dark days of his life.
Through much prayer and hope she was able to cope
As God soon took away G.T.'s strife.

The world is a much better place today
Because of our Corporal Grays.
His legacy lives as more young men give
Their lives for the American way.

I salute this great soul, today Heaven's hold,
And know that eternity's gained.
He abides up above in that mansion of love,
And one day there we'll remain.

(Dr. Cravey's Eulogy at G.T. Gray's Funeral Service)

Today, America grieves a fallen hero, one who gave himself
willingly during World War II, entering the Army in May of
1941. His dog-tag numbers were 34082396. He trained at
Fort Benning, Georgia, Fort Bragg, North Carolina, 90 days
in Louisiana, where he never slept in a bed but wherever he
could find a spot on the ground. From there he returned to
Fort Benning and later to Indiantown Gap, Pennsylvania, to
prepare for overseas. He and his fellow troops were then
shipped off to Southampton, England, and then to North Africa. He served in General Mark Clark's Fifth Army in the
894th Tank Destroyer Battalion. The next time that G.T. slept
in a real bed was April 1945--27 months and 22 days later!
He fought in the Tunisia Campaign against the German General Irwin Rommel's Afrika Corp. Many battles were fought
as well as the infamous Battle of Kasserine Pass in February
of 1943. Many Americans and Germans lost their lives, approximately one in every four! There was also the Italian

front in which G.T. fought in the invasion at Anzio and the Naples-Foggia campaign and on to Rome where they fought in the Rome-Arno Campaign and later the terrible four-month battle of Monte Cassino. They entered Rome on June 4, 1944. A picture of G.T. and another soldier on their tank was in Life Magazine. Other battles ensued for this young soldier and his comrades. Winters were so cold out in the open while fighting that the men put skull-caps on their heads and their teeth literally rattled. When they breathed, their breaths froze and their chests hurt. G.T. did most of his sleeping on the cold, hard floor of his tank, catching a wink or two whenever they were not engaged in battle.

Needless to say, G.T. grieved over the countless men he had to gun down from his tank as well as on the field. He knew, however, in his heart of hearts, that he was doing what was right against the atrocities of the German military. He fought for freedom for all people, against the evil regime. As Ecclesiastes 3 states, "To every thing there is a season, and a time to every purpose under the heaven: A time to be born, and a time to die; a time to plant, and a time to pluck up that which is planted; a time to kill, and a time to heal; a time to break down, and a time to build up . . ."

In these latter days at hospice, G.T. would often be found with his hands folded in a prayerful mode upon his chest, and you could overhear him mumbling words that were usually indiscernible. I feel that he made his peace with God over this very traumatic issue. He was one of our great American heroes and will be sadly missed.

On a lighter note, G.T. was full of frivolity, always keeping you in stitches with his wit and common-sense wisdom. For instance, he always said that he wanted to be buried at Walmart so at least Betty would come by and see him from time to time.

His work back home included years of motel management at the Mandalay here in Lyons, manager of the Elks Club, and 18 years as a correctional officer at Georgia State Prison in Reidsville, Georgia. He made a difference in this community and area as long as he could and was always loved and admired by those around him. His family today rises up in unity and calls him BLESSED. All of our lives will be better because of this great man.

Our many thanks to the countless ones who sat with Betty and G.T., the Community Hospice folks who were superb in every way through his latter days, the Home-Health nurses who came and cared for this great American, to the friends, family members and others who prayed daily for God's Will to be fulfilled. You have all given this family strength, hope and encouragement.

Let me close today with a new salute I've learned that we all can use in the future whenever we are wanting to say thank you to someone in the military. It is from sign-language and goes like this: (hand across heart and unfold it forward).

Oh, God, our heavenly Father, we are humbled at your greatness and goodness shown to this precious and loving family, and especially to our dear G.T. Gray through these long years of his life. Thank you for allowing us these years to know him and love him. Thank you for bringing him through the many years of service safely so that his story could be told. May your continued grace and mercy be with this family and with us all as we strive to move forward in faith to accomplish thy holy will. May we, too, be found worthy in the end and thus, be received into thy glorious kingdom above. In the Name of the Father, the Son and the Holy Spirit. AMEN.

Emmaus Walk #72

Many of you will have already heard of or have been on a "Walk to Emmaus" weekend. I was invited to attend Walk #72 with forty-one other men from the middle Georgia area from Thursday night through Sunday afternoon. The setting was at an old historical Methodist campground near Vienna, Georgia. The pilgrims on the walk stayed in rustic cabins which surrounded the tabernacle. Each hour was filled with planned activities of a religious nature and emphasized spiritual growth. This "walk" became, for me, the single most spiritual experience of my life, sharing my faith and growth with those forty-one other guys. Our lives would never again be the same.

My wife attended the next Women's Walk and also felt spiritually renewed and revived. Together, our views of spirituality have changed - for the better. We have a new focus in our spiritual walks and a host of Emmaus friends who are there for us.

Accountability is a key element in Emmaus. Local churches are just not oriented in this way, so we are missing a key element that could serve to make the church stronger.

Please accept the invitation to attend a Walk when a sponsor calls or asks. It could very well be the most important choice of your life.

Special Interest Groups

I am concerned over the power that special interest groups seem to have in society today. One case in point would be how less than 5% of Americans have professed homosexuality but their power and ability to push their agendas upon us has grown tremendously. Now, it seems, most every TV series and movie has to have a "gay" person in it to represent that 5% of the public who choose such a non-Biblical and unnatural lifestyle. I am appalled that we have allowed this to happen. How can we continue to teach our children moral principles when they are seeing the acceptance of this way of life whenever they watch TV or go to the movies?

The proverbial "Pandora's Box" has been opened and the question becomes, "How can we undo what has been done? How do we put this 5% or less back in the box?"

Our Judeo-Christian morals and values *must* prevail in teaching society against the act of homosexuality. We cannot waver or fail for this 5% of the American populace are unfailing in their quest to become accepted. What will you do?

Hall Trees and Dreams

I recently built my niece, Kayla, an oak Hall Tree with bench for her wedding gift. It was a real joy to do this for her and to see her acceptance of it when Renee and I delivered it to her home in Warner Robins, Georgia. She and her husband, Phillip, have been married now for almost a year, and they live in a very nice home in a former Peach orchard.

After we delivered the Hall Tree and placed it in Kayla's dining room area, we were given a tour of their home. In the kitchen I noticed that the sink probably needed replacing sometime in the near future. Kayla and Phillip both told me that the disposal had never worked since they had been there. Being the handyman I am, I reached my hand down through the disposal flaps and immediately discovered the problem. A small wash cloth had slipped down into the mouth of the disposal and had become trapped and entangled in the blades. I pulled hard on the cloth until it unraveled and I pulled it out. I then turned the water on and hit the disposal switch and it hummed and purred like it was brand new! Kayla and Phillip were amazed and reacted as though that was the very best gift they could have received, far surpassing the gift of the Hall Tree which took countless hours in tedious construction! Are there things in your life that may be a little clogged up and forgotten or rendered useless? Have you unfulfilled dreams that before were rendered unreachable that could possibly be recovered now? A little faith, perseverance and work should suffice in realizing those dreams again and bringing them to fruition. Never give up simply because life threw a dish cloth into the mix. There are ways to overcome such impediments if we'll work at it.

I'm sure that Kayla and Philip will remember "Uncle Charles" whenever they turn on their disposal in the future. Such simple things seem to matter the most!

Realize those dreams today by opening your head and your heart to the possibilities awaiting you.

When My Ship Comes In

What do you do when the opportunity of a lifetime finally comes along when you least expect it?

I've been writing Gospel songs since the age of eighteen (after my Christian conversion) and have recorded forty-two albums of my original music since then. I have several songs published by other companies and released nationally and internationally by other singers or groups, but have never had a national release with me singing. Songwriter/singers always dream of a national release with *their* songs and *their* vocals.

Finally, at fifty-nine years of age, I've been offered a recording contract by a prominent publishing and recording entity in Oklahoma. They will choose which song/s will be promoted on radio and the album will be nationally distributed. They will promote me and help secure concerts for me to perform.

Here's the perplexing dilemma: although I have always wanted and dreamed of the day this would happen, it comes at a time in which I'm much older, less inclined to travel, my voice is weaker, my profession as a minister comes first, and I'm nearing retirement. What would you do? The answers do not come easily and the complications are numerous. I'm facing a deadline for signing the contract so I need to respond quickly.

I've always told folks that when my ship finally does come in, I'll probably be at the airport!

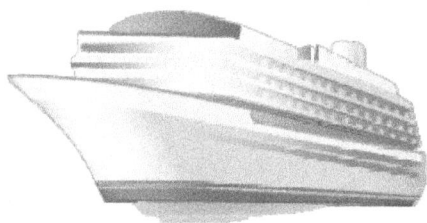

Making Production

My mother worked tirelessly for years at two different shirt factories. She would sit for hours behind a sewing machine and sew together a certain part of a shirt and had to make "production" in order to keep her job. Making production never ceased; once you've made a thousand pieces in a day to reach production, the factory then ups the production rate the following day for an additional number of pieces. The cycle is endless and very stressful. Your life becomes similar to that of a zombie--sitting there hour after hour doing one mundane task over and over until either the lunch or end-of-work bell rings.

What an analogy of life this is. We work hard our entire lives but it never seems good enough, and so we work harder or just drop out of the race. The stress of making production is just too much for some people, so they choose a different route.

Our present rat-race, keeping up with the Jones's, making production - all serve in taking life from us instead of bringing us life. Jesus came to give you life. Turn to Him and find the salvation that will restore you and bring meaning and happiness to an otherwise mundane existence. God bless.

Saving Private Ryan

The year was 1944, Omaha Beach in Normandy, France. Captain John Miller and his platoon were given orders to find and rescue Private Benjamin Francis Ryan, who had already lost three other brothers in the war. After discovering this great loss to the family, the Commander of the Army decided to have the one remaining son rescued and returned to his mother at any cost. It cost the lives of several soldiers, including Captain Miller, but the rescue was successful. Lying wounded and dying on the battlefield, Captain Miller pulls young Private Ryan near and whispers his last words to him: "Earn this!" In these two words, Captain Miller implies the great losses of life paid for Private Ryan's rescue.

In the heart-rendering final scene of the movie, Private Ryan and his family are in the military cemetery where many of the men in that platoon were buried. While standing in front of Captain Miller's grave, the aging Ryan begins weeping and asks his wife if she thought he had "earned" it. What a moving and very touching moment. Could any of us ever truly "earn" the sacrifices paid for our freedom by others?

In the gospels, Jesus compares our salvation with several illustrations, including the "Prodigal Son" story, the "Lost Coin," the "Lost Sheep" which had strayed from the fold - - all symbolizing how the owner, the father, the shepherd had dropped everything in order to recover that one thing which had been lost. Jesus ultimately gave His life upon the cross for our salvation. "Earn this!"

Omniscient, Omnipotent, Omnipresent

I first encountered these three words in seminary at Emory University in Atlanta, Georgia. Since that time, they have helped me better understand God and His presence in our lives and in the world. Let me share my understanding of them with you and illuminate their meaning for my life. Psalm 139 will be our guide as we move from one word to the other. David divides his psalm into three distinct six-verse sections which will highlight each term.

Psalm 139: 1-6. God is "**Omniscient**," which means "all knowing." He framed the world and the universe long before you and I became an afterthought. He was before us and will be long after our departure. Scientists can never put God under a microscope and seek to discover His nature for our finite minds could never wrap themselves around such an infinite Being. Suffice it to say that our God knows all and is always few steps ahead of us. Once we can accept this, the sooner we can discover the peace of God which surpasses any human understanding.

"O Lord, thou hast searched me, and known me. Thou knowest my downsitting and mine uprising, thou understandest my thought afar off. Thou compasseth my path and my lying down, and art acquainted with all my ways. For there is not

a word in my tongue, but, lo, O Lord, thou knowest it alto-
gether. Thou hast beset me behind and before, and laid thine
hand upon me. Such knowledge is too wonderful for me; it is
high, I cannot attain unto it." (Psalm 139: 1-6)

Psalm 139: 7-12. God is "**Omnipotent**." God is everywhere
at the same time. He's busy in the jungles of Africa and yet,
dwells within our hearts. His very nature is to be everywhere
-- all the time! How could our small minds ever comprehend
such a God? You and I are like grasshoppers when com-
pared to the Omnipotent God; yet, many like to equate themselves with God. God possesses infinite power, so limitless
that He not only spoke and the universe was brought into being through His love, but He also made Himself a servant
(through Jesus Christ) and ultimately sacrificed His life to
bring our hearts unto Himself.

"Whither shall I go from thy spirit? Or whither shall I flee
from thy presence? If I ascend up into heaven, thou art there:
if I make my bed in hell, behold, thou art there. If I take the
wings of the morning, and dwell in the uttermost parts of the
sea; Even there shall thy hand lead me, and thy right hand
shall hold me. If I say, Surely the darkness shall cover me;
even the night shall be light about me. Yea, the darkness hi-
deth not from thee; but the night shineth as the day: the dark-
ness and the light are both alike to thee." (Psalm 139: 7-12)

Finally, God is "**Omnipresent**." This refers to the unlimited
nature of God and the ability for Him to be everywhere at all

times. God was in the beginning, in the middle, and will be in the End. There is no escaping Him. He is in our innermost thoughts. He knows and counts every hair upon our heads. He even numbers all of our days upon earth. Even our secrets are privy to God. For those who believe in Him, God actually takes up residence (through the Holy Spirit) in the human heart and mind and is there for all time.

"For thou hast possessed my reins; thou hast covered me in my mother's womb. I will praise thee; for I am fearfully and wonderfully made: marvellous are thy works; and that my soul knoweth right well. My substance was not hid from thee, when I was made in secret, and curiously wrought in the lowest parts of the earth. Thine eyes did see my substance, yet being unperfect; and in thy book all my members were written, which in continuance were fashioned, when as yet there was none of them. How precious also are thy thoughts unto me, O God! How great is the sum of them! If I should count them, they are more in number than the sand: when I awake, I am still with thee." (Psalm 139: 13-18)

Therefore, beloved, God knows all things, Sees all things and is everywhere all of the time. He is the master and Creator of all through His wonderful power and holds all things together. To God, in all three forms, be the glory forever. Amen!

That's What Friends Are For

Sam Lamback, a good friend of several years, told me recently that he was in his shop over the Christmas holidays making a wooden toy for one of his grandchildren and had one of my CDs playing on his stereo while he worked. It thrilled me to know that he cared enough about my music to have it on. He and I have served on several "Walk to Emmaus" weekends as band members and as clergy counselors. His love for music is tremendous and equals mine. He is a great bass and banjo player and is also very adept at writing poetry.

As a friend and mentor, Sam and I were meeting to discuss my future. With much concern and care, Sam would challenge my train of thought and lead me to consider other possible scenarios. I left our meeting with enthusiasm and hope. That's what friends should do for us -- give us hope and encouragement but also help us face reality.

Jesus desires to be just such a friend. His ways and thoughts should and will challenge us if we will allow Him room in our hearts. His answers will not always be in the affirmative; sometimes He will say "NO" in order to move us in a new direction. God's desire is for our completeness. Friends who never challenge us aren't very good friends!

I feel certain that I could call Sam at any time with a need, and he would reach out and help. I hope that he knows I would do the same for him! That's what friends are for.

Color Blind

I was in Lab Tech school in Atlanta, Georgia, and had completed six months of training. My mother had always wanted me to be a doctor, but I talked her into this route instead. It was a twelve-month course and the school would even find a work position for me after graduation in a local hospital or clinic setting.

The Vietnam War was in full swing in those days, and several of my high school friends had already been inducted into the military, so I figured my draft number would soon be called. I stopped at a Navy Recruiter's office one day while on my way home from school and discussed the various offers he put forth if I would go ahead and enlist. He confirmed that my number would soon be called and that I would probably have to serve. He also told me that, with my six months of Lab training, he could request ship duty for me instead of combat and I would do lab work on the ship to identify and process the wounded or fallen soldiers. I felt that I would be foolish not to accept his offer, so I signed up. I would go over to the induction center on Ponce de Leon the following Tuesday for a physical.

On that Tuesday, I entered the Induction Center with fear and trepidation for what was about to happen. During the full day's testing, all modesty was left at the door. At one point, over 300 young men were lined up along both walls facing each other, without a stitch of clothing on!

From one test to another, we all moved like cattle through the rank-and-file. One of the last tests was designed to determine color-blindness. A man sat behind a table and held up cards, one after the other, which had colored bubbles. One was supposed to make out either numbers or letters in the bubbles but I couldn't see anything but BUBBLES! The man stamped a "failure" mark on my card and I proceeded to the next test, the final one of the day. I left there with a card to return to my recruiter which clearly showed a rank of "4-F," meaning that I had been rejected due to color-blindness. Since I had signed up for the Navy, it was most important that I not be color-blind.

The following week, I met with the Navy Recruiter again and he assured me that if I would be willing to take the test over again in a few weeks that I would be accepted. Having escaped the big draft, however, I decided to remain in school without the fear of my number being called.

This was God's way of saving me for the ministry which I would later be called in to and have served for the last thirty-nine years! As the Bible states, "Many are called but few are chosen" (Matthew 22:14). Guess my color-blindness saved me for the greatest draft of all!

How Much You Care

"People don't care how much you know until they know how much you care." I have heard this quote for many years and do not know its original source, but its message is so true. We could care less about how much knowledge a person possesses but we never fail to notice how much they care.

Mr. Ryals lived at the top of Pot-Liquor Hill in my hometown of Helena, Georgia. He raised chickens, pigs, and had a two-acre garden from which he would share the abundance of with folks in need each year. It would be nothing for him to hear about a family down on their luck and to put together a ham or chicken and some vegetables and carry to them. Mr. Ryals never asked any questions about the family's dilemma and never took any money for his many acts of kindness. He had been blessed with much and was willing to share his bounty.

I used to work for Mr. Ryals as a young guy and would pick peas, pull corn, or cut okra for him at $5.00 a day--a very fair price in the last 1950s and 60s. He was truly a caring individual and will always be remembered for his love to others.

I remember Mr. Ryals sharing with me one day while we were working as to how he had to quit school in the first grade to work on the family farm. His father had died, so he and his brothers had to work the farm in order to survive. As it turned out, he never went back to school. In essence, it wasn't an education that taught him how to be a caring person but the hard knock school of hardship and experience. For years, before I knew about his lack of education, I thought that Mr. Ryals was the smartest man alive!

Memory Loss

"Memory is the mother of all wisdom." - Aeschylus, 430 BC
I write to record as much of the past as possible, realizing the fragility of the future and that day when I may be unable to recall certain events of my life. I write for my children and grandchildren to leave behind a record of my life. It may not be of much interest to you, but it will be invaluable to them one day.

I have ministered to many Alzheimer's patients over the course of my life as a pastor and know how fragile life becomes when one can no longer remember the past or those around them. It is very hard on family members to watch as their loved ones slip into the foggy future and lose memory and communication. As of yet, we do not return from that journey. This is why I constantly encourage people to journal their daily lives, leave a record behind while still able, and to share with loved ones as much as possible. It is sad to watch the progression of this disease, so please do not wait until you're diagnosed before you attempt to do something about it. Start today to leave behind a record of your life for time and posterity. Your family will be most thankful.

My wife accuses me of having "selective memory," choosing to remember only the good things of importance to me and forgetting other sides to the story. We all may actually be guilty of this.

Some years back, I attended an all-day seminar on Alzheimer's in Macon, Georgia, led by doctors and nurses from the Carondolet School of Management in Arizona. This is a Catholic Medical facility which has studied this disease long before a name was given to it proper. At one point, we were told that one should never treat or talk to an Alzheimer's patient as we would to a child. The patient can hear you, just as before, but simply cannot respond as we desire them to. Treat them as usual with respect and never demean them by speaking childishly.

Our memories are precious and hold the history of our lives. Be faithful and diligent and begin that process of recording the past for others. They will be most glad you did.

To Be President

"If you have faith as small as a mustard seed, you can say to this mountain, 'Move from here to there' and it will move. Nothing will be impossible for you." - Matthew 17:20-21, NIV

I grew up in a day and age in which anything seemed possible and within reach if you simply had the faith to bring it to fruition. I was the kid who never accepted defeat but strived to find an alternative way to accomplish that which seemed impossible.

Growing up poor, one has no other place to look but UP, so I was always looking up and forward to the day when I could be or do as others around me had done.

I knew that if one wanted to be President, he could. It would take getting a proper education and putting forth the efforts of perhaps running for a local office first and then following that with larger aspirations until he was accepted into the right socio-political arena. From there, he could launch his move.

President Jimmy Carter, from my home state of Georgia, became President through improbable odds. Jimmy and his family were dirt-farmers in Southwest Georgia, but Jimmy never allowed that to stop his bid to become President of these United States!

There's the kid who struggled through Little League as a pitcher with very little promise. Yet, he had the dream and vision of pitching for the Atlanta Braves one day. So he continued to throw and pitch his way through American Legion ball and in high school until he developed a slider that hardly anyone could touch. By his senior year in high school, he was the starting pitcher for his team and went 12-2 that year, catching the eyes of a couple of scouts.

There he was at last, some six years later, following four years of college at the University of Georgia, and two years in the minor leagues, standing on the mound pitching for the Braves! His dream and desire had come to fruition, but not without believing in himself when others doubted, and putting forth a lot of work and effort.

Most of my teachers called me "incorrigible" in elementary school because I always did things differently than the rest. I was always questioning "Why not?" of the teachers when clear answers could not be given.

It was in high school that I finally encountered an English/ Literature teacher who saw the potential in my vain attempts at poetry and writing. She encouraged me to keep writing, and so I did. Because she believed in me, I compiled volume after volume of writings and poetry in those early days.

Today, I am President/Founder of The Society of American Poets, an international organization. We compile and print a quarterly poetry magazine, THE POET'S PEN, which is shipped to many national and international poets, libraries, and bookstores. The Society has been in existence for the past 26 years and continues to grow.

I also created a book publishing company, IN HIS STEPS PUBLISHING, which has, to date, published over 400 books. All of this from that "incorrigible" kid who daydreamed in school.

I guess I've always had faith in myself and what I could accomplish if I would simply apply myself. I do not consider this as vanity, but faith.

In Hebrews 11:1, we read the following: *"Now faith is the substance of things hoped for, the evidence of things not seen."*

There you have it -- my credo: I can do anything with a little faith, even faith as small as a grain of mustard seed!

Friend, never up or give in. Stay the course of your dreams and work hard to bring them to fruition. Believe in yourself, even when others do not. Do not expect life to simply drop something great into your lap one day. Work for it. By faith in yourself and in God, you can accomplish the impossible!

Smarter Than a Fifth Grader

I've just watched a young lady make a fool of herself on the TV show, "Are You Smarter Than a Fifth Grader?". She was given the simple question, "Two countries border the Great Lakes. The United States is one of them. What is the other?" She could not answer the question and used her dad in the audience for help. He said "CANADA!" and the girl screamed for joy!

This young lady graduated from college recently with a 3.6 grade point average and is working in Retail Marketing. Tell me, how did she possibly make it through high school and college without knowing the simple answer to this question? And yet, she stumbled through each question on the show and failed to win anything except a consolation prize.

Today's educational system is failing. I'm really not sure what they're teaching these days, but it's certainly not education. I call it "The Dumbing Down of America." We used to be the smartest people on Earth (here in the U.S.), but that has now changed. China is currently graduating physicians, engineers, technicians and others at a rapid pace, far ahead of us. In fact, their graduates are now being hired by U.S. firms! How humiliating. Japan, that country we defeated in battle, now excels the American Educational System. India sends merchants to the U.S. to operate our convenience stores!

Mexicans are doing most of our manual labor for us! We tolerate their citizenship status so our corporations can have good workers. What is happening to us?

We have to remember that we are one of the youngest nations on earth, and as such, must continue to excel and to move forward in technologies and science. But it begins with each of us and our attitudes. We must recover the dreams and aspirations of that young nation again and revamp our educational systems and stop offering "free rides." Where do we begin?

Copeland's Cross

As you may have gathered, from some of these articles, I am an avid woodworker. I enjoy the fresh smell of pine shavings, maple, oak or cherry sawdust as I rip through lengths of board feet to cut the needed units for a new project. Wood glue, nails, brads, sanders, routers and hammers make up my arsenal of finishing tools. Shellac and wood stains help bring the wood's color to a shiny and beautiful finish. It is with great pride that I stand in front of a finished product and see the face of the person I've built it for. It is deep contentment I feel when I know the person loves the finished work of art.

Having completed one work, I begin thinking about the next project or how to improve upon the one just finished.

One of the most priceless wood projects ever completed was not created by my hands but by a dear, long-ago departed friend and fellow woodworker, C.M. Copeland of Fitzgerald, Georgia. In 1975, C.M. called me and said he had just finished carving a gift for me. I went immediately to his woodshop and discovered the beautiful wooden cross necklace he had carved for me from a Cypress knee. Having carved hundreds of crosses in the past, C.M. stated that this one was the first to form a natural cross pattern in the grains of wood, a most unique occurrence!

C.M. made his crosses and other small carvings to sell at craft fairs on weekends, but this one was given freely to me by the artist, himself. He only asked that I wear it from time-to-time and remember him in prayer, which I have done for years, long after the woodworker's departure from this life.

C.M. Copeland lives on through his small gesture of a cross which has attracted many admirers through the years. Priceless to me are the teething marks of both my children when they were very small (Angela, now 34; Jonathan, now 30). It will one day be passed to my son when I make my departure. Hopefully, the story of its artist will continue on for many more years.

Our Great Artist and Creator formed and fashioned each of us with His hands into the priceless and treasured beings we are today. We were not rejects or cast-offs but His greatest work of art. Therefore, let us make the greatest use of what we have been given.

The Bucket List

Morgan Freeman and Jack Nicholson star in one of my all-time favorite movies, "The Bucket List." The story is built around two cancer patients who have been given a few months to live and are roommates in the same hospital where Nicholson is the Administrator. Freeman is an automobile mechanic.

Freeman puts together a "Bucket List" of things or events he wants to accomplish before he "kicks the bucket" (dies). When Nicholson discovers Freeman's list, he begins to revise and add to it. Together the two take off to see the world and to complete the listed items. Nicholson is a very rich man, so he pays the ticket.

During one of their various trips, the two are found sitting atop one of Egypt's famous pyramids. Freeman is telling Nicholson about an old Egyptian lesson on how one gets into Egyptian "heaven." He states two profound questions that must be answered affirmatively in order to enter Paradise. Nichoson asks what the two questions are and Freeman responds:

(1) Have you found joy in your life?
(2) Has your life brought joy to others?

These are two vital questions for each of us to answer. Regardless as to your perceived future destination, it is important that our lives are lived in such a way as to answer these key questions in the affirmative.

Take the first question - "Have you found joy in your life? Can you truthfully say that you have found joy or inner peace in your lifetime? This is really the eternal question, isn't it? The quest for peace, love, joy, and happiness dominates our lives as we associate with and live out our existence in the presence of others. If we seek the solitary life, we are less likely to experience these sought-after entities. It is usually in community that we find joy through our association and relationship with others.

In the movie, the rich Nicholson has spent his entire adult life busily seeking the almighty dollar. His days had been filled with business meetings, schedules, the stock market, etc. Cold, calloused, emotionless days filled his life. He had lost at love by ignoring the needs of his ex-wife. He had ignored his only child, a daughter whom he had lost contact with because of his infatuation with work. Because of his failure to commit to the relationships around him, Nicholson's character had failed in producing any real "joy" in his personal life.

When the gurney carries you away at death, how will your life reflect in light of this question? Will you have found joy in your life or just a fleeting and meaningless existence?

What is YOUR present joy? Mine happens to be found in the sweetness of my two grandchildren, my relationship with my wonderful and supportive wife, my two loving children, my personal relationship with Jesus Christ, and my friendship with so many caring and loving friends. Yes, I have found an abundance of joy in my life and will die a happy man, whenever that day arrives!

When Nicholson is unable to answer affirmatively to the first question, he asks (in frustration) what the second one is. Freeman then asks Nicholson, "Has your life brought joy to others?"

That's the infinite question for us as well. Has our earthly existence brought joy to others? Have we made an impact for goodness, love, joy, peace . . . in the lives of those around us? Will we be missed when gone? Will others grieve our passing? We should strive daily to live our lives for others, to invest ourselves in bringing happiness and joy to them, creating and maintaining meaningful relationships.

Nicholson's life had been lived through manipulating others in his business and personal relationships. He's empty inside and has nothing to show for the life he has lived. What a sad commentary this evokes!

Nicholson finally discovers joy in his life when he visits his estranged daughter and discovers a beautiful young granddaughter who smiles and hugs her grandfather for the first time! Peace and love begin to flow into his life at this point, and leads the viewer to believe that he has finally found his purpose for living.

Make today count. Bring joy to others and find LIFE in the process!

The Treadmill

Due to my shortness of breath, my cardiologist recently requested a few tests for me which included a treadmill regimen to ascertain how quickly I gave out of breath. The test would also monitor my blood pressure before, during, and after the test, to determine any irregularities. My results were fine, even exceeding a "normal" rating, but we are awaiting other tests to determine the cause of my shortness of breath.

While on the treadmill, the speed of my walking was constantly increased and then I was put on an elevated track. My legs were shot after the test and hurt for the next several days, showing how "out of shape" I've become at 59. I know what I need to do, but am I willing to do it? I need more exercise, a heart-healthy diet, and a change in lifestyle. It will take a great deal of commitment for me to get into the shape necessary to please my cardiologist.

Aren't we all on life's treadmill? We're trying to pass the test but often fail due to our lack of commitment to a proper and healthy lifestyle. When will we make the move to begin living a happier and more healthy life? That's the pressing question for us today. What will it take to convince us to begin? A heart attack? Hospitalization? A debilitating illness?

Decide today to get off that treadmill and begin living the

abundant life you know you should in order to be happier, more excited, more enthusiastic about living. The choice is totally up to you.

We're Having a Baby

Angela Marie Cravey was born in Fitzgerald, Georgia, on July 4, 1976, on a Sunday afternoon. She was an 8 pound 12-1/2 ounce baby girl filled with joy and quickly became known as "Little Miss Independence" because of her birth on our Nation's Bicentennial. She has definitely lived up to that billing for the past thirty-four years, always acting very independently and sure of herself.

Renee and I had prayed for a child during our first four years of marriage, but with no success. On a Saturday evening, I remember vividly having a dream (while napping) of a beautiful blonde little girl and I called her "Angel" in my sleep. I was dreaming out loud and Renee heard me and awakened me when I kept repeating "Angel." She wanted to know who "Angel" was, so I then shared the dream with her and told her that we were going to have a beautiful little blonde-headed girl and would name her "Angel," for she would be God's Angel to us.

Two weeks to the day, Renee did one of those packaged pregnancy tests and we rejoiced at its "positive" results! One week later her gynecologist confirmed the pregnancy. Nine months later, on July 4th, we held that beautiful, blonde baby in our arms and gave her the name, "Angela," which means "a gift from God," our little "Angel."

This same little Angel has brought us much joy by bringing two new angels of her own into our lives -- Benjamin Matthew and Meghan Marie!

I have always heard that God assigns an angel to each of us. I have mine, do you?

Polygamy

I've just finished reading a cover article from my February 2010 issue of National Geographic magazine on "Polygamy in America." The article features the Joe Jessop family. Joe and his family are members of the FLDS (Fundamentalist Church of Jesus Christ of Latter Day Saints). Joe has five wives, 46 children, and 239 grandchildren! I've found it most difficult to support one wife, two children, and now two grandchildren. How in the world could Joe support so many and remain sane?

The Holy Bible is clear that we should be the husband to ONE wife or the wife to ONE husband. There is no room for compromise on the issue.

What Joe Jessop is doing is "self-indulgent," building his own little religious world in which he is King, Lord and Master. This is completely unbiblical and simply NOT RIGHT! No matter what rhetoric or theology they purport, it is not of a Biblical nature and is thus, ungodly.

There are many such cult groups in our world today basically devised by man and his egotistical desires. Many suffer at the hands of such leaders (i.e., Jim Jones and Jonestown; the Waco Cult). When will we realize that only Jesus Christ can lead us into "true" family and community with one another?

Chance Encounters

I first encountered the Reverend David Ogletree at First United Methodist Church in downtown Atlanta, Georgia, on July 3, 197, in the office of the pastor, Dr. Robert Ozment. I had sought financial help from the church because my school tuition payments had not arrived and my rent was due. Furthermore, I had no food to eat. With nowhere left to turn, I turned to this large metropolitan church, hoping they could help. This encounter would help transform my life.

I had been given an audience with Dr. Ozment in his office that day to ascertain my needs. Reverend Ogletree, the church's youth minister, was brought in as well and also Reverend Carl Standard, the Associate Pastor. After hearing my need of $100.00 to get me through the next week, they presented me later with $250, more than I had asked for. Reverend Ogletree also invited me to their young adult class party a week later, and I attended and felt my heart "strangely warmed." A few weeks later, Dr. Ozment baptized me on a Saturday afternoon in that beautiful old sanctuary. Reverend Ogletree was also present as witness to the event.

From those early young adult classes, the generosity of the church, the compelling sermons by Dr. Ozment, and the counseling of my dear friend, Reverend Ogletree, my life began to take on new meaning and purpose. I started a Bible study class at the Church's Home for Business Girls every

Thursday evening. We had four attendees the first week and grew to over 40 in a month! Facilitating this study would eventually confirm my call into ministry. Many of the young adult women accepted Christ during those meetings as we continued to grow well beyond 50!

Over the course of the next year, I returned home and accepted the call to ministry though my local United Methodist Church. I would not encounter Reverend Ogletree again until recently at Epworth By the Sea, a Methodist Retreat Center on Saint Simons Island, Georgia. He now works in retirement at the Arthur J. Moore Methodist Museum there. I knew him the moment I saw him and we hugged each other and did a bit of reminiscing of my time in Atlanta and how he had played a large part in helping to transform my life. Although nearly forty years had passed since our last encounter, it seemed like only days ago to the both of us.

There are special people in life, with whom we have chance encounters, who will enable us to grow and mature in our faith if we will allow them. Reverend David Ogletree will always hold a very dear and precious place in my heart. He reached out to a little nineteen-year-old country boy in a large, metropolitan city of strangers, and befriended me forever!

May each of your chance encounters be blessed and transforming in some small way as you make your way down the hectic and often frustrating avenues of life. Be blessed.

Foreign Matter

It's 45 degrees as Terry and I crawl around the blueberry bushes to cut out the foreign growths such as small maples, briars and undergrowth before spring growth and blossoms begin. It is vital to do this for the plants. If left untended, the foreign matter would take over the acres of blueberries within a short while and eventually destroy their productivity.

Luke 13:6-10 records a parable shared by Jesus which depicts a man who had a fig tree that had not produced fruit for three years. He tells his gardener to cut down the tree for it was taking up space in the garden. The gardener begs to try a restorative act of digging around the tree and putting fertilizer in the soil. If it did not produce the following season, then the gardener promised to cut it down.

Does your garden need pruning or clearing of foreign matter? Are there things creeping into your life that may slowly have their way in you or possibly even destroy you? Sin is the culprit which seeks to separate us from the Savior and will sap away our happiness and joy. Jesus came to take away our sin and to cleanse us from unrighteousness. If we will yield our lives to Him, we will, in essence, purge our garden (life) of any foreign matter (sin) and be freed from the bondage of sin and death.

Famine

There is a menacing famine in America today. It is relentless and cruel and brings even the strongest of persons to their knees. It lurks among us daily and seeks to devour whatever it can. The weak-minded do not stand a chance in its wake. It destroys by slowly taking away what is needed for survival. Call it whatever you will, it is still a famine, a dearth that eventually brings death. It can be the lack of food, contaminated water supplies, a contagious disease, a ravaging flood, an horrific earthquake or hurricane, or even a more base disease such as Alzheimer's.

My dear friend has been closer to me than a brother in recent years but has now crossed the Meridian line of health and is slowly moving into an Alzheimer's state of mind. Little things we've noticed lately lets us know that things are getting worse. There is a famine going on in his mind and he is frustrated and anxious to speak about it, but his thoughts will no longer form into sentences with any meaning. The other morning, following breakfast with his wife, he looked up from the table and said, "It's so good to see you again," as though he was greeting an old friend instead of his beloved wife. The family realizes the dilemma and is beginning to prepare themselves for whatever happens next. If it runs its usual course, it won't be long until my friend becomes unable to communicate. This is the most difficult part for the family members. I pray sincerely for God's healing grace, but few recover from this dreaded famine.

What are you hungry for today? For what does your soul thirst? What disease or illness is keeping you from discovering the fuller life?

There is that beautiful story in the gospels of a Samaritan woman who approached Jesus one day at the city well. Jesus asks her for a drink of water and she, recognizing Jesus as a Jew, responds by saying that Jews and Samaritans did not mix in public and here he was asking her for water. Jesus responds by telling her that if she really knew who he was, she would have asked of him for water and he would have given her "living water." The woman then questions Jesus by asking what he would have used to draw the water with from the well since he apparently had nothing in hand. Jesus then states, "*Whosoever drinketh of this water shall thirst again: But whosoever drinketh of the water that I shall give him shall never thirst; but the water that I shall give him shall be in him a well of water springing up into everlasting life.*" The woman then bids Jesus to give her that "eternal water" for which we all yearn. The drought is over, the famine has been lifted, she has been restored to fullness of life.

Isn't that exactly what we all yearn for -- living water? Aren't we seeking that needed commodity each day of life? We know what Jesus has to offer to every thirsty pilgrim, but are we willing to accept it? How happy we would be to receive that thirst quenching drink of living water!

May you never suffer through a famine or drought in your life. May things always go your way. May the road of life be always easy for you, and may your always walk in the sunshine and not the rain. These are all well-wishes, but not realistic, are they? Fact of the matter is that we will all endure hardships, pain and suffering in this life, but there is One Who offers eternal life and LIVING WATER! Receive it today and end the famine in you.

Pain

I recently had my big toenail removed by a Podiatrist! It took three shots before my toe was numb and the doctor proceeded with the removal. My face was covered with sweat and I felt nauseous when he began the procedure. I gripped both sides of the bed I was lying on and gritted my teeth through the ordeal. Man, I have never before experienced such pain as that day! That night, as soon as the numbing medication wore off, I began to experience a new kind of pain as the toe began to recover. I couldn't stand for anything to touch the toe and could barely walk on that foot. For days the pain lingered with me, the toe throbbing endlessly. I pray that I will never have to go through that ordeal again for as long as I live!

I was reading recently about the reality of "Phantom" pain and how people who have had organs, arms or legs removed still feel pain in those extremities. Our scientists and physicians have researched enough to now know that the pain is real and that it actually comes from the spinal cord and brain. It is a most difficult sensation to treat. Your leg is no longer there but you still feel it as though it was present.

And then there are "growing pains." Growing pains are relegated to children and are untreatable. The child simply grows out of the pain as their muscles and joints mature. It is part of life and growth itself that causes such pain.

Pain is an important process in life. Without the existence of pain, an untreated illness or disease may go unnoticed until it's too late. Pain is there to serve us and to let physicians know what our problems are. And thus, pain is a paradox, it serves both good and bad purposes.

I have a dear friend with Osteoarthritis and this friend has what is called "Chronic pain." This is pain which never subsides or goes away. There are medications to help ease the pain but none to alleviate it completely. One simply has to suffer through its severity.

And then there is the mental pain we suffer over the loss of a loved one, the stress of daily life, or a disease of the mind which alters our thinking and behavior. This can be the most devastating pain of all and I've seen it literally destroy people and families.

I was reading recently in Psalm 55 and ran across this verse dealing with pain. "My heart is sore pained within me: and the terrors of death are fallen upon me" (Psalm 55:4). Apparently the psalmist is suffering from the absence, or perceived absence of God from him in his hour of need. It is a most painful experience in our hearts and minds to be without the soothing Lord of our Salvation. He is the salve of comfort and healing. He alone can bring that healing balm of Gilead. Turn to Him today.

The Fear of Desolation

Picture a barren wasteland where little of life exists. Everything is in ruin and only a few brush plants are thriving. Sand completely covers the area and the sun beats down at over 110 degrees. The nights are cold and harsh. This would certainly not be an ideal location to build your dream home!

In Proverbs 1:24-27, we have a discourse from God which illuminates the state of unrepentant man living in the certain fear of this kind of desolation.

*"Because I have called, and ye refused; I have stretched out my hand, and no man regarded; But ye have set at nought all my counsel, and would none of my reproof: I also will laugh at your calamity; I will mock when your fear cometh; When your **fear cometh as desolation**, and your destruction cometh as a whirlwind; when distress and anguish cometh upon you."*

There are only a few opportunities in which God knocks upon the door of our hearts to allow Him in. Our refusal leaves us in a state of desolation; our souls are barren of spiritual life. He has called but few have answered. His hand has been stretched out in our barren state but we would not take it and find life. Instead, we have refused sound counsel and have laughed at those who seek to lead us to the Savior.

The choice has always been ours to make, still many refuse to follow.

In a very realistic way, we are in that barren wasteland of the soul if we are not living the life God purposed for us. The results of living this kind of life brings calamity, fear and destruction. Then we wonder why bad things are happening to us! But wait, there is more to this scenario.

"Then shall they call upon me, but I will not answer; they shall seek me early, but they shall not find me: For that they hated knowledge, and did not choose the fear of the Lord: They would none of my counsel: they despised all my reproof." (Proverbs 1:28-30)

The desolation continues after our refusal of God's call. We find ourselves in utter despair and then cry out to the Lord only to find that He does not answer. We seek Him but cannot find Him. We are lost in our indifference. Everything goes wrong. We live in desperation to hear His voice once again calling to us in our fear.

"Therefore shall they eat of the fruit of their own way, and be filled with their own devices. For the turning away of the simple shall slay them, and the prosperity of fools shall destroy them." (Proverbs 1:31,32)

By turning to our own devices we refuse to listen to sound reason. God is calling but we refuse to hear. Many have heard His prompting but have chosen to lead their own lives, falling eventually into the fear of desolation.

But wait, there is hope! If we would only turn to God at His calling, our lives would become fruitful and flourish.

"But whoso hearkeneth unto me shall dwell safely, and shall be quiet from fear of evil." (Proverbs 1:33)

I remember so well, nearly thirty years ago, a young lady coming down to the altar at the close of our evening service. As I knelt with her and took her hands in mine, I asked if she needed special prayer. Her response was that she felt certain that God was calling her to follow Him into some ministry of sorts, but that she was not quite ready. She loved her job and was not willing to give it up at the time. I remember feeling that her life was held in the balance at that moment, then to discover the following afternoon that she had been involved in a tragic and life-ending car wreck! My words at the funeral sought to bring consolation and the peace of Christ to the congregation, but I knew in my heart-of-hearts that she had refused the call of God upon her soul that night at the altar only two days prior. How tragic! How desolate!

Friend, are you dwelling in the wasteland of fear and indecision? Are you putting off the call of God upon your life? I implore you to turn to Christ today and receive His fullness and glory. Do not wait until the time is "right," for it may never be again. "Today" is the day of your salvation.

A Time For Every Purpose

Ecclesiastes 3:17 - *"I said in mine heart, God shall judge the righteous and the wicked: for there is a time there for every purpose and for every work."*

You perhaps remember the old saying that "Every dog has his day." How true I have found this to be. There is nothing we do that will not be found out sooner or later. We may go for a season, but the past will return to haunt us at some point in the road. We cannot outrun God and His righteous judgment. The justice of God will prevail in the end. Both the righteous and the wicked will be have their day.

I have been angry lately over something a person has said about me that wasn't true. It was cruel and hard-hearted and actually sought my demise. The person was self-serving and did not like my authority and, so, rebelled against me. I'm sure this has never happened to you! My anger was righteous anger, knowing that this person did not act out of their love of Christ, but the exact opposite. Many months later, I have come to grips with my anger (never once shown towards the person) and have moved on in my life. However, the person who sought to destroy me will still have to deal with God's judgment at some point. It is not my desire for this person to suffer, but God will be the one dealing with their actions.

"He who justifies the wicked, and he who condemns the just, both of them alike are an abomination to the LORD."
(Proverbs 17:150)

I have since received a letter of apology from this person, but it was a little too late in coming to undo the damage the person had done to me. I feel that it was a vain attempt to alleviate the suffering the person was going through, both mentally and medically. That person will have to deal with the aftermath of their wickedness with God. Only God can bring them again to a state of peace.

Every dog does have his day, sooner or later. May God bless mine accuser and restore him unto Christ.

Excessive Baggage

"Let us lay aside every weight, and the sin which doth so easily beset us, and let us run with patience the race that is set before us" (Hebrews 12: 1).

One of the reasons why most young Christians cannot move forward in their new life in Christ is because they carry so much "excessive baggage." We are reluctant to let go of our former lives, old habits, questionable friendships, and a host of other "baggage" that eventually weighs us down and prevents the full life in Christ. It is imperative that the new Christian rid him/herself of this baggage and move forward to run the race of life serving Christ if we are going to be effective for the kingdom of God.

A friend of mine had a major habit when he first gave his heart to the Lord and I tried to explain to him that it would suffocate his new life if he continued in that habit. I thought then, from that point on, that he had given it up until I encountered him some three years later only to discover that he had allowed the habit to drain his spirituality. He was only a semblance now of the person he had become when he first surrendered to Christ. The habit had brought him down and had even brought more "sin" along with it!

Finally, my friend surrendered - heart, soul and mind - to the fullness of Christ and his life has really taken off with new meaning and direction. He walks a different walk and now talks a different talk, using the old habit as a point of reference for others who may be suffering from the same. His ministry has become fruitful and has multiplied tremendously since giving up the weight of the old habit.

What is weighing down your reluctance to live the full life? What impediments or baggage are you carrying that prevents you from moving forward? There is a race of life set before you and you will not win unless you totally surrender those habits and sins that beset you. Confess those sins today, name them one by one for what they are worth, and lay them upon the altar of God's grace. And then, pick yourself up, dust yourself on and get back in the race! Christ is counting on you.

Perpetual Backsliding

"Why then is this people of Jerusalem slidden back by a perpetual backsliding? they hold fast deceit, they refuse to return. I hearkened and heard, but they spake not aright: no man repented him of his wickedness, saying, What have I done? every one turned to his course, as the horse rusheth into the battle. Yea, the stork in the heaven knoweth her appointed times; and the turtle and the crane and the swallow observe the time of their coming; but my people know not the judgment of the Lord.." (Jeremiah 8:5-7)

Perpetual backsliding, a familiar problem among the Jewish nation of Israel. Time and again, throughout scripture, God warns the children of Israel of their backsliding ways yet, they heed not and fall further into sin and disgrace. In God's wrath and anger their land is taken from them over and again, a perpetual problem as we read through the Old Testament scriptures. WHEN will they learn? WHEN will WE learn? It is an age-old question posed to every believer.

Jeremiah, the prophet of God, talks of how the people of Israel seem to be like horses that rush into battle. How ridiculous is that sight? It reminds me of the tactics of our American Civil War and how the two flanks (north and south) would line up on either side of a field and charge into battle without any cover or protection. To me, that sounds ridiculous and fatal. With guns and cannons blazing across that field from both sides, the chances of survival were very slim to none. The horses were even more vulnerable in those battles, and so are the children of God who rush headlong into each day without the protection and wisdom of Almighty God on their side.

Another analogy that Jeremiah uses in this passage is that of storks, turtles, cranes and swallow knowing exactly when their time is coming and make their annual pilgrimages (migrations) to specific places at specific times. Why, Jeremiah asks, can Israel not see the writing on the wall and turn from their wickedness to God, their only hope of salvation? Over again they had been warned of impending danger, yet they refused to hear the warnings and to obey their God.

It is almost time for my beautiful little hummingbirds to return from wherever it is they go for the winter. It is truly amazing how we can almost predict the week of their departure each year and the week of their sudden return to our feeders which hang from our front porch. If this tiny little creatures know and can sense the timing of such migrations, then more so should every human being. Yet, says Jeremiah, we have turned our ears and eyes from God and will not heed His warnings. As a result, we suffer greatly and fail in battle. We are devastated by our enemies who are prepared and ready and overwhelm us with might.

Just a thought in closing: could this be why Israel continues to be in constant conflict with the rest of the world? Christians believe wholeheartedly that the land of Israel belongs to the Jews as a gift from God. America, a Christian nation, has literally spend billions of dollars in helping Israel survive as a nation because of our beliefs that Israel still belongs to the Jews. Biblically speaking however, when one reads the Old Testament, the land was often given to other clans and tribes of people in battles fought against the Jews because of their constant rebellion and turning away from God. The Palestinians are one such people who inhabited the Holy Land before Israel became a nation again in 1948. The great Dispersion had separated the people of Israel to all parts of the world and now a call to return to their homeland has seen thousands of Jews coming home to Israel. But yet, there's the dilemma over what to do with the Palestinians who still feel that the property "rightfully" belongs to them. The new Israel was mandated by the United Nations, the United States and Great Britain, so what little hope do the Palestinians have of reclaiming THEIR homeland? Their people suffer greatly each day and are unable to secure the bare necessities for life. They have been pushed, over and again, into little pockets of the Holy Land region, where life is hard to sustain. Fences have been erected as a sort of prison for the Palestinians in order to try and keep the Jews safe from their enemies.

O.K., here's the question: Is it right to ignore the needs of the Palestinians in Israel because of some Old Testament "right-of-passage" that the land belongs eternally to the Jews? How can we continue to support the atrocities of the Palestinians by the people of Israel by pumping even more money into the Jewish economy each year to make certain they do not fail again? Read Jeremiah's warnings again and then re-read the Old Testament scriptures pertaining to the Jews perpetually backsliding and having their land taken from them. Do they really deserve a nation-state at the hands of the Palestinians? That question continues to be at the heart of every battle fought between these two entities and the spilling of precious blood on either side. It will never be resolved until the Jews completely annihilate the Palestinians and run them off, or Americans and others finally see that Palestine deserves to be an independent nation as well with support from other nations for their survival.

Perpetual backsliding. That's the problem, isn't it? When will we recognize the call to return to our roots and to follow the clear path of salvation God has prepared for us? In the animal kingdom, there is no question of seasons, migrations, and following their inner spirits. Why should there be with us? Be well.

When Your Faith is Strong

"And, behold, there came a leper and worshipped him, saying, Lord, if thou wilt, thou canst make me clean. And Jesus put forth his hand, and touched him, saying, I will; be thou clean. And immediately his leprosy was cleansed."
(St. Matthew 8:2,3)

Is your faith strong enough to see you through the toughest of times? Take this man in our scripture who had contracted leprosy, a terrible disease of the skin which leaves one with lesions, boils, and huge growths that are very unsightly and gross to others. In this particular age, lepers were excommunicated from their families and friends and had to live out their remaining lives in the hill country with other lepers of similar fate. Their "uncleanness" was their doom. What a tragedy for anyone!

This particular leper did not allow the other lepers, nor his ex -communication, to stop him from seeking help. He wanted to return to wholeness and happiness with his family and friends and had the inner faith and strength to believe that one day it would happen - his cleansing, his healing. One day he hears of this man called Jesus and leaves his leper friends behind to seek Jesus out. He finds him surrounded by the multitudes but pushes forward to seek healing. This leper actually bows down before Jesus and begins to "worship him."

He recognizes the fact that Jesus could heal him if he wanted to. Why wouldn't He? Seeing that kind of faith, Jesus simply puts forth his hand and touches the leper (an unheard of maneuver!) and heals the man *immediately*! What a Savior!

Jesus, realizing the process for a cured leper in Jewish society, instructs the leper that he should go directly to his priest and show himself as being cleansed and offer the gifts required by Moses for restoration into the family (Leviticus 14:3,4,10; Luke 5:14). It was a fairly detailed process which also included the sacrifice of blood from a lamb. Isn't it ironic that a sacrifice of blood is also required for the remission and forgiveness of OUR sins and unrighteousness? Jesus supplied that blood on the cross of Calvary. Is your faith strong enough to receive it for cleansing and renewal? God bless you, my friend in Christ.

The Great Commission

My first true calling, months after my Christian conversion, was to the ministry of serving Christ. At that time I did not know exactly "what" that ministry would be, but in the months to come, it became very clear to me that I was to minister to people in a local church setting. I began serving a part-time charge of three churches while maintaining my full time job with Juvenile Court Services where I worked as Georgia's first "Community Worker." While on that job, I was given the responsibility of identifying with the youth assigned to me by the courts and finding the right plan to propose for adjudication. It would then be my responsibility of making certain the youth followed the plan. If not, then they would be brought back into court and sentenced to a juvenile correctional facility. I could identity with most of them, for I had been arrested at thirteen and had spent two and one-half months in the Telfair County jail with two other juveniles before we were given probation.

I loved my work with the youth and made great progress in helping to lead many of them to a new life with purpose and direction. I did this for two and one-half years while serving my three churches on the weekends. I also played in a Christian Rock Band with four other guys and we shared our faith in Christ to many youth groups in those days. At the same time, I was writing songs at a voracious pace and the band played several of them in concerts.

In 1974, I felt the call to a deeper ministry (without the band, without juvenile court) of working full time in a local church. I was appointed to a wonderful little church in Fitzgerald, Georgia, where we made great strides with the people. I baptized several new members and our little congregation grew mightily during my three years there. I also had to attend college in order to move forward towards ordination and full conference membership as an elder in The United Methodist Church. My life was now fulfilled and God's Spirit confirmed it; I was where He wanted me to be.

Many Christians are still roaming about as zombies trying to figure out what it is that God would have them do with their lives. I think that Jesus' final words to His people before His ascension into Heaven is all too clear in Matthew 28:19,20: "Go ye therefore, and teach all nations, baptizing them in the name of the Father, and of the Son, and of the Holy Ghost: Teaching them to observe all things whatsoever I have commanded you: and, lo, I am with you alway, even to the end of the world. Amen."

There you have it in a nutshell. What does God require of each of us in this Great Commission? We are to teach nations and individuals about God and His love and plan of salvation. We are to baptize them into the life of Christ. We must teach them to observe God's commandments and to assure them that God is with them and for them at all times.

Since my early call, I have traveled the world teaching other nations of people about Christ and His plan, building churches in foreign countries by physical labor through the many work-teams I have led, sharing the gospel in prisons, youth development centers, nursing homes, hospitals and wherever folks would listen. I am not being vain but merely showing you what one person, committed to Christ, can do only by the power and grace of God.

What are YOU doing in His kingdom today? Still sitting and wondering? Get busy. There is much work for you to do. Prayerfully consider your calling today and God's Spirit will do the rest as He opens new horizons for your life. Others are waiting to hear the gospel from you. Be faithful to the calling.

Walter "Bud" Nickel - 7/12/09

Bud Nickel started working when he was eight-years-old in a Pittsburgh Bakery and has worked most all of his life serving other people. You could say that this was his purpose for living -- to serve others. Early on he joined the military with exemplary service to God and country. It was during this time that he confronted a beautiful young lady named Kitty here in the Lyons/Vidalia area when Kitty was 14. Family members have shared with me that Kitty remarked back then that Bud was a "good looking guy." She married him at 16, a week or so before her 17 birthday and has loved this wonderful man ever since.

In his latter years of work, prior to retiring, Bud served as a prison counselor. I'm sure that those he served would vouch today for his sincerity, love and concern shown to them by this very gentle and loving man. He was truly a friend to all and a blessing.

He was a good daddy -- a loving husband, and one of the nicest men I've ever met. That smile of his was very contagious and brought him many blessings along the way. His children and grandchildren rise up today and call him "blessed."

I spoke with Bud by telephone last Monday morning. He described for me his room and the beautiful view he was given the opportunity to witness by looking out his window. He described the lake and the ducks and birds that flew over, and even the hawk that kept swooping down on the water to catch fish! I asked him if he needed anything and he said, "Brother Cravey, I have everything I need. I'm content just waiting for the next step. Don't worry 'bout me; everything is fine. Just keep me in your prayers." I assured him that we would and that God would continue to hold him in the greatness of His glory and power. I prayed with Bud over the phone before we hung up and I had a great peace.

Thursday, Bud's new heart finally arrived. It wasn't the one we all expected, but it was the greatest of all hearts--the very heart of God. God knew that the road ahead would be rough and long and brought this blessed pilgrim the rest he deserved. He fought a good fight; he kept the faith. He has won the final victory with Christ.

Ecclesiastes 3:11 states that *"God has planted eternity in the human heart."*

In the beautiful trilogy of the "Lord of the Rings," two little hobbits, Sam and Frodo, are sent off into an evil world to save it. Calamities happen to them; they escape many encounters by the hair on their heads; the dark world has a hold on them, but they are determined to press forward to their calling. At one desperate point in the saga, Sam turns to Frodo and states, "I wonder what sort of tale we've fallen into?"

Isn't that life? Isn't that our question as well? Ours is a story
yet to be told. I remember those beautiful lines from an innocent Forrest Gump when he stands beside his dying mother's
bed and asks her the question: "Mama, what's my destiny?"
Her response was those now famous words, "Forrest, life is
like a box of chocolates; you never know what you're gonna
get."

And so it is with Life. We never know what the next bend in
the road will bring, but we, like Sam and Frodo, keep pressing on, deeper and deeper, into this life and its circumstances,
doing our best to find our destiny, our place in the overall
scheme of things. But there is One much greater Who knows
the entire story of our lives and has promised to never leave
us nor forsake us in our hour of trial but would, in all ways
prepare a means of escape for us, even in our darkest hour.

I firmly believe that our Savior came on Thursday to receive
our dear brother. There was nothing that any of us could have
done to have changed that. Those final days of his life were
to prepare us for the journey that took place in that hospital
room. The saga of his earthly life came to a close, opening
that beautiful realm of God's heaven to a much deserved pilgrim who is now HOME.

Where will the saga of our lives take us? What events will
transpire to shape us into the persons God is calling us to be?
It has yet to be determined how we will live out the remaining days and years of our lives, but He Who holds the keys to

life and death will stand with us and never leave us. HE will be our shield and our defender and will maintain His promise of eternity with Him if we are faithful, for "He has planted eternity in the human heart."

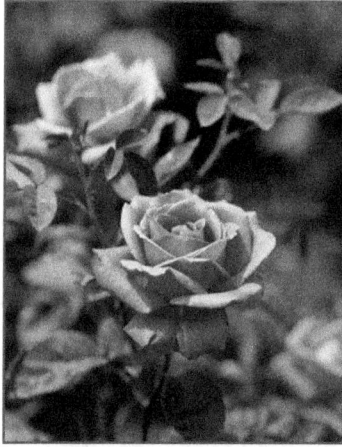

Examples of Faith

Hebrews 11:1 - *"Now faith is the substance of things hoped for, the evidence of things not seen."*

We all look through a glass darkly. We cannot see beyond the horizon of our vision to the depths of our souls, but God can. We believe in things that visibly do not exist. And so FAITH in God is our reason for believing. It is wonderful to know that there are those listed in the Old Testament whose lives and faith were tested. We look to them as examples of how we should live. This discourse is intended to list some of them and what they endured because of faith.

In Hebrews 11:4, Abel is our first example. This story comes to us directly from the Garden of Eden, well (actually) outside of the Garden. Cain, Abel's brother, was enraged because Abel offered unto God a "more excellent sacrifice than Cain, by which he obtained witness that he was righteous." Perhaps Cain's heart wasn't in the right place, and out of anger he rose up and slew his brother in the fields. We should never allow our envy of others to destroy our faith. Regardless of the sacrifices of others, we should always give our best and do our best for God.

Next, Enoch is mentioned in verse 5 as having been translated (taken up into Heaven). The beautiful part of this passage is that "he pleased God." Do you please God by the life you live? Are you faithfully serving Him daily?

"But without faith it is impossible to please him: for he that cometh to God must believe that he is, and that he is a rewarder of them that diligently seek him." (Hebrews 11:6)

Noah is mentioned next in Hebrews 11 as one who received a warning of the impending flood and prepared an ark, as God required, and fulfilled the quest before him. As such, he *"became heir of the righteousness which is by faith."* (verse 7)

Abraham was asked to pack up all of his belongings and to move to a new place without question. He obeyed and received a great inheritance from God. We should never question the Spirit of God when we are called upon to move-up, move-out and beyond. Go!

Again, another faithful servant, Sarah, conceived a child beyond child-bearing age. She was "judged" as "faithful" by God. May we be found righteous and faithful by God when He returns.

"These all died in faith, not having received the promises, but having seen them afar off, and were persuaded of them, and embraced them, and confessed that they were strangers and pilgrims on the earth." (Hebrews 11:13)

There are others mentioned in this great chapter, but suffice these few witnesses to attest to God's faithfulness. Here is a short listing of some of the hardships they endured:

-subdued kingdoms
-wrought righteousness
-obtained promises
-stopped the mouth of lions
-quenched the violence of fire
-escaped the edge of the sword
-made strong out of weakness
-waxed valiant in fight
-turned away armies by might
-women received their dead raised to life again
-tortured in various ways
-endured cruel mockings and scourgings
-in bonds and imprisonment
-stoned
-cut in two . . . (from Hebrews 11:32-37)

What more can we say of those who have set the example of our faith? The standard is before you. The road can be tough and trying, but faith makes it bearable. Faith is the answer.

Notes for High School Seniors

There are three main things you can do over this Summer to help prepare you for college:

1. Read one or more of the books on the first year of college and getting ready for freshman year.
2. Many colleges offer study courses or student-success courses your first semester or during summer orientation. Take one!
3. Do an honest self-appraisal of your strengths, weaknesses, and goals. What areas do you   struggle   with? What are your stressors? How might you deal with those stressful times?

Think these through and come up with a game-plan to manage your future.

There will be many <u>temptations</u> in college which can get you off-course, but if you keep true to the golden rule of all things in moderation, you'll make life as easy as possible.

Be willing to talk to your professors, librarians, family and friends for support. The professors and librarians are paid to be there to talk to you and assist you. Many students will experience fear, anxiety and get overwhelmed by school and pressure.

"Stress" can be the "spice of life" or "the kiss of death," depending on how we cope with it.

"Two men looked through prison bars;

One saw mud, the other stars!"

Be "over-prepared" for your tests, class discussions, and presentations. My son, Jonathan, graduated from a small county high school as Valedictorian and Star Student and immediately found himself behind in his freshman first semester! College will be much more challenging than your high school experience and will be much tougher than you imagine. Don't wait until you fall behind--prepare ahead of time for EVERYTHING!

DO NOT PROCRASTINATE! PLAN TO BE EARLY TO EVERY CLASS!
As the saying goes, "Yesterday is a canceled check, tomorrow is a promissory note, but today is ready cash. Use it!"

To master our time, we must have a goal, a plan, then take action!

Plan now to take responsibility for your life.

Proverbs 22:6 - *"Train up a child in the way he should go: and when he is old, he will not depart from it."*

Seventy (70%) percent of young adults drop out of church for at least one year following high school. Please do not be a statistic! Stay strong in your faith and it will help see you through. Find a church near your college or university where you can "plug-in" and get involved. I found church to be a supportive and strong influence in my college years.

Hebrews 10:24-25a - *"Let us think about each other and help each other to show love and do good deeds. You should not stay away from the church meetings, as some are doing, but you should meet together and encourage each other."*

Finally, be faithful in all that you do. Others will attempt to convince you to "try this" or "try that." Please do not be gullible enough to give in. Live faithfully and you'll survive and grow stronger for the world that awaits you. Be well.

To My Dear Friend, Roy

A dear friend departed this week and left a vacant spot in my heart! His name was Roy Funk from Tifton, Georgia. In his obit, his wife included one of his favorite sayings:

"God doesn't owe me anything!"

Roy was always full of life and never made excuses, nor listed a number of regrets. He lived life to its fullest every day and gleaned as much as he could from 24 small hours.

Would that we all could live our lives as did Roy—never expecting any handouts from God, but always working and toiling for that which was worthwhile. Roy would say that God gave him life and it was up to him to live it! I like that attitude and hope you do as well.

I've known a lot of folks in my lifetime who seems to feel that the world owed them something. They were always looking for a handout without putting forth the toil and sweat to secure it. What could have possibly given them pleasure in life if they spent every waking moment trying to "get" instead of "give?" It had to be a miserable existence for them.

Be well and full of happiness. Life is too short to fret the little stuff!

Comfortless

Comfort is when my friends give me moral support and encouragement and ministers to the needs of my heart. During a time of frustration my wife consoled me through her loving touch by assuring me that "this, too, would pass." What a wonderful gift we can give to others merely by expressing or interjecting a bit of joy into their lives through our loving and caring attitudes!

It was 3 AM at the Medical Center in Macon, Georgia, when I walked into the ICU waiting area. I had been awakened by a church member who called to let me know that a dear friend had been in a terrible automobile accident and was on the verge of dying. She told me not to come at such an hour but to be in prayer for her friend. I rushed to get dressed and wiped the matter from my eyes and proceeded across town to this large medical facility. The streets were almost bare of other vehicles and the cold enveloped me as I drove towards my destination with every thought being a prayer of supplication for this dear person on the brink of death. I had never met this person before but my church member considered her as her best friend.

As I walked into the waiting area, my church member noticed me immediately and came running to me. She grabbed me and held on for dear life, sobbing and almost inconsolable. When she finally released me, I took her hands in mine and we sat down and I listened to her retell the events of the evening. I could tell that just by my being there brought her comfort, knowing that she did not have to face what was to come in the ensuing hours alone. We prayed together and asked for God's Holy Will to be done in her friend's life. She then asked if I would go into the ICU and have a prayer or blessing upon her friend and I agreed to do so. The nurses were so kind to me by allowing me entrance at such an hour, but they knew that the young lady was in very critical condition.

When I pulled back the curtain at the foot of her bed, it startled me to see her. Her face and arms had been mangled in the wreck and she was heavily sedated to ease the pain. The nurse said that she was in and out of consciousness, so I softly made my way to her bedside and asked if I could pray with her. She responded with a small nod of her head. I placed my hand upon her forehead and prayed a prayer of healing grace and mercy upon her, putting her completely in the Lord's care, and followed that with the twenty-third Psalm of David. She smiled a broken smile at me following the prayer and I ensured her that her friend and me were just outside and that we would be praying there for her.

As I left her bedside, the nurse told me that she probably wouldn't make it much longer for she had massive internal bleeding and damage to her liver and lungs. Knowing this gave me then the impetus to deal with my church member and help her to prepare for what was ahead.

"Preacher, thank you so much for coming, but you really don't have to stay," she said as I approached her again in the waiting area. "You have been so kind to come when I called, but you've gone above and beyond the call of duty."

I really felt like God had brought me there to help console and comfort my church member, so I stayed with her and shared scriptures of comfort and consoled her as best I could.

It happened around 5:30 am that morning. The nurse came out to where we were sitting to let us know that the young lady had just passed. Her family, who lived several hours away, would be there shortly, but at that moment it was only the two of us to wait for them to arrive with the heavy hearts of such a loss.

I was able to minister to the family, once they arrived, and agreed, at their insistence, to preach her eulogy in a few days. To this day, that church member always reminds me of that night and how I had responded to her in her hours of grief and mourning. She will never forget the comfort I brought to her.

Jesus shares with his disciples those beautiful words in John 14:18 where he states: "I will not leave you comfortless: I will come to you." I'm not Jesus or an angel, by any stretch of the imagination, but my friend still, to this day, says that when I walked into that waiting room that night it was like she was seeing an angel appear.

The comfort of Jesus comes in many different forms. Are *YOU* a comforter?

Virus

One of the many hazards of working with computers is the eventual "virus" which downloads itself onto your hard drive and begins to wreak havoc. Ultimately, if left untreated, it will attach worms or trojan horses to your files and leave your computer inoperable. Millions of dollars are spent annually to rid our computers from such viruses and restore them to usefulness. Sometimes the old system has to be discarded and a new one purchased. And to think that these viruses are created by computer nerds wanting to be destructive and to disrupt the flow of information. They get a tremendous rush when they hear of "their" virus attacking systems on the daily news. If you haven't been attacked yet, brace yourselves for, in all likelihood, you are primed to receive one!

Viruses are all around us. I recently read on the internet about a deadly virus attacking the cricket population in Louisiana, the nation's leading cricket producer of chocolate-covered crickets, fish bait, and God only knows for what other uses!

And then there are the viruses that attack the human body. Our granddaughter, Meghan, recently suffered through a week long flu-bug that made the little five-month old difficult to deal with and left her parents frustrated and very concerned.

In the real world, we have computer programs to help protect our computers from costly viruses and medications to help protect our bodies from severe viruses, but none of these are perfect. There are no catch-all cures and this leaves each of us vulnerable and susceptible. It is often a very helpless feeling when we are attacked.

What about our souls? Do we have a virus protection program which will prevent sin from entering our hearts? Are you truly safe? Only through the blood of Jesus can our souls be cleansed and made new. Turn to Him today for that much-needed protection He alone offers.

In The Family

My friend in Christ, Tom Jackson, came up through the School of Hard Knocks. As a former drug addict, Tom's life was headed down a one-way street. He was one step away from death when he was transformed at a church service by the hand of God. Since then Tom has excelled as a true disciple and faithful follower of Jesus Christ.

I've recently published two books for this youth minister of eight years. His latest is entitled, "In The Family," and is a great little guidebook for new converts to Christianity. He and his team give these out at high schools, youth meetings, prisons, and other venues where they have an opportunity of sharing Christ. The book inspires and directs new converts on the next steps of their journey with Christ. It is well written and full of encouragement for new Christians to "stay" IN THE FAMILY.

Tom is the CEO, President and co-founder of FlameThrower Ministries, Inc. His heart is to see this generation set on fire for Jesus and change the world by the power and demonstration of the Holy Spirit.

Tom holds regular meetings for youth in an old converted store front building in McRae, Georgia, and they even have a praise band, a Christian dance team, and a dedicated core group of witnesses all willing to share their faith to others. Hundreds have been received into the family of God through this wonderful and powerful ministry.

I'm one who is delighted to have Tom Jackson in the family of God! Let us pray for him and the many others who are helping lead our youth into a meaningful relationship with Jesus Christ today. It is a daunting task, but my friend Tom is up for the challenge! May his numbers increase.

Close Calls

I watched her as she ran right through the red light, barreling along in her old clunker, challenging anyone to try and avoid her. Luckily, I saw her in enough time to slam on my brakes and avoid the near-collision. She never turned to notice the havoc she had caused due to her recklessness!

And then there was the big Buck deer dashing from the woods at a break-neck speed and right out in front of my car. I hit the brakes just in time but nearly lost control of the vehicle! It could have been devastating.

We all have such close calls every day and aren't usually prepared for them. They take us by surprise and often when we are most vulnerable. Would that we could live in some kind of bubble where we're protected from all that life hurls at us, but we aren't. Life is a constant chance encounter with every close call.

A Christian's only hope is in the saving grace and tender mercy of Jesus Christ. Pain, affliction, suffering and heartaches will come and go, but the Peace of Christ remains forever!

New Strings on An Old Guitar

Several years back a dear friend left me with a 1947 Gibson acoustic guitar. He had bought it new at the close of WWII and had never learned to play it; it became just one of his many possessions gathering dust in his closet. He called me over one night and said it was mine if I wanted it! Are you kidding me? Indeed, I wanted it, and so would any true guitarist! A guitar like that one is almost priceless on the market today. It was handmade by skilled craftsmen and is a true work of art.

Because of the Gibson's pristine nature, I do not use it when performing. I have a fairly new Taylor that I play instead. Yet, the mellow tone of the Gibson cannot be copied on another guitar; it is an amazing sound.

I took the Gibson out the other day and restrung it with a new set of silver strings. After tuning it, I played a few chords and was overwhelmed by its beautiful, crisp, clear, melodious sound. And then I remembered Chad Culpepper from Warner Robins, Georgia, who departed long ago and left me with such a beautiful and timeless instrument! He will always be remembered for this fantastic gift.

At Chad's graveside service, I mentioned the old guitar and Chad's gift of it to me before giving the final committal and

Benediction. I talked about its beauty, clarity, and how the sound permeates one's soul and how Chad's life had intersected mine and we shared that perfect gift. That sound will live on for years to come! Thanks Chad for such a wonderful gift.

Chimney Sweepers and Life

We've just had our chimney cleaned by a professional chimney sweeper for the first time in five years. Each season I had put this off, thinking that the chimney was fine, but the chimney sweep told me that, had we waited much longer, the house could have potentially burned down due to the accumulation of tar and silt!

Life is that way, isn't it? We trod along at a vicarious pace each day and fail to see the "clutter" which gathers around us and within us. It accumulates over the years of neglect and poses a real and certain danger if left untreated.

We could all use a "Heart Sweeper" to help us cleanse and prepare our hearts anew. But will we realize the dangers and seek professional help in time?

I've learned my lesson, thank goodness, and have established an ongoing annual sweep of our chimney. I've also taken care of the "heart" situation as well. How about you?

Ben's First Solo

Our grandson, Ben, took his first solo bike ride last Sunday afternoon without Granny or Gandy (that's me) holding on! With his little feet (five years old) he pressed the pedals and would go a few feet and stop, a few feet more and stop. He finally worked up enough confidence to go the distance of our yard, about 50 or 60 yards. We celebrated with him and clapped our hands for his accomplishment. You could see the pride rising up in his face and through his actions. He was now "on his own."

I remember some thirty years prior teaching his mom how to ride her first bike. I finally gave her a push and turned loose of the bike and she took off and has never looked back since! She can and still does anything she sets her mind to, and I'm proud to have had a part in her development.

From training-wheels to solo, we're all in a learning curve in life and need the constant help and encouragement from others to help us get started. What seems impossible at first soon finds us soloing through life! Be well.

"Who Touched Me?"

She made her way through the raucous, bustling crowds of the city streets where people had gathered to hear from the eloquent speaker. Crowds were boisterous and rowdy, and she found it difficult to move through the masses with her feeble and debilitating illness. She had been to various doctors in recent weeks, but had no relief from her pain and anguish. She was unable to work to provide even the barest of necessities for herself and that made her quest to reach this man all the more important. She just had to see what he had to offer her, although now, seeing the great numbers of people lined-up to see him, if she could even get close!

As she struggles past, she bumps into person after person and feels the pain surging through her broken body. If only she could get to him, she felt that he could do something to help restore her. Each step, each movement forward increased her faith.

Finally, she was near enough to the speaker to hear his words of wisdom and so, while on her knees, she crawls and reaches forward and touches only the hem of his garment. She is quickly brushed aside by the crowd, but then something truly amazing happens . . .

"And when he saw her, he said, Daughter, be of good com-

fort; thy faith hath made thee whole. And the woman was made whole from that hour." (Matthew 9:22)

That's our story as well, isn't it? We were diseased and infirm due to the sins of our lives, but Jesus saw our despair and reached down into our hearts with His saving grace and restored us. What a Savior! What a friend!

Final Arrangements

My friend in Christ, Gloria Pate, recently called to check on me and in the course of our conversation, she shared with me what she had done the day before. She and a relative had gone down to the local funeral home and had made her final arrangements, picking out a casket, vault, burial plot, and dealing with such items as pallbearers, minister, the opening and closing of the casket, etc. She said that she had felt a burden lifted after the arrangements had been made, and she now had an inner peace about it all. Her mother passed a couple of years ago and Gloria was left alone. Having taken care of this now brought her great consolation.

Are there things you need to take care of today that may be weighing heavily upon your soul? Are there unresolved issues, relationships, or plans you've been putting off? Why not get busy today and take care of those things while they are fresh on your mind and heart. As with Gloria, I'm sure you'll find a great inner-peace once you've done this. God bless you all.

Lake Independence

On my first mission trip to the Central American country of Belize, I had the privilege of helping dig the foundations for a new church. While there, I remember putting one of my guitar picks into the foundation before it hardened, and other team members put some personal trinket of theirs into the mix as well. Fifteen years later, we returned to do work in another area of Belize and dropped in for a worship service with the people of Lake Independence Methodist Church. We were pleased to witness a crowd of over 200 that morning, and they asked us to give witness during the service, which we did. Pictures of the various work teams hung proudly in the vestibule and our first team was at the very top. There I was, young in the ministry and missions, standing with my team and several of the faithful church members. The photo was faded a bit, but not my memories of that event.

After services concluded, two ladies approached me and said they remembered me and my team with fondness because they had both accepted Christ during the services we held that week under a tent! Both of them now teach Sunday School at the church and are affecting the lives of many children in that neighborhood of Belize City. My heart leaped for joy as they shared their testimonies and witness with me.

You and I will never completely know how many lives our

faith has affected through the years so we should always remain faithful to the calling of Christ.

My next trip to Belize will be in the Spring while on a Carnival cruise with my wife, but this time as a common tourist, but one with such fond and loving memories of past missions there where we labored with those beautiful people to help bring more of the gospel of Christ to them. The church has grown tremendously in its outreach and witness, and I'm most thankful for having had the opportunity to serve.

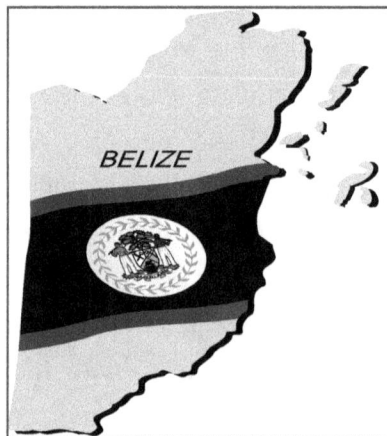

Evolution and Man

O.K., here's my brain question for all of our scientists out there and believers in evolution: If man supposedly evolved from Apes, then why are there still Apes? The theory just doesn't fly!

Why are we so prone to believe such theorists when the Biblical story of creation has never been proven false? If we would look at scriptures with open minds, we could clearly see a progression of evolution from Day One of creation through Day Six. One also has to remember that in 2 Peter 3:8 the words are recorded: *"But beloved, be not ignorant of this one thing, that one day is with the Lord as a thousand years."* If a thousand, then what about a million, or two? There's plenty of room for interpretation.

Fact of the matter is that we are always trying to disprove the Word of God by scientific and logical thinking, but in vain. We are mortal; God is immortal. We are human; God is Spirit. How could we possibly ever think that we, mere mortals, can find the mystical answers to the questions of our universe? Why is that even important?

I settled the questions in my mind at the age of eighteen when I gave everything I knew about myself to everything I knew about God. That relationship has grown tremendously over the years and today I'm at perfect peace with knowing that God's Word stands alone, apart from any scientist's inquisitive questions.

One should only read about the Tower of Babel and the attempts of that day to know God's wrath and anger whenever we try to become like Him. The people of that day were separated out to various nations, races and color. Will we make that mistake as well?

When the Iron is Dull

I went off half-cocked this morning to the Blueberry field with trimmers and cutters unsharpened. It was a long morning because the blades would not cut through the toughest of small trees growing between the blueberry trees. It is important that we rid the field of these pesky little saplings so that the blueberry can grow properly and that people can pick the berries without hinder. I should have known better, but I was in a big hurry for some reason. Again, I have learned my lesson the hard way.

Ecclesiastes 10:10 states: *"If the iron be blunt, and he do not whet the edge, then must he put to more strength: but wisdom is profitable to direct."* It all begins with a sharp blade and someone responsible enough to keep it sharpened. Ecclesiastes states it well: if the blade is not sharp then one must put forth more strength in getting the job done. Wisdom, on the other hand, comes from the experience of knowing that one can do little work with a dull blade. He who is wise will take the time to do the necessary tasks before a work is to be done. Life is more profitable if we take the time to "whet the edge" and to make sure that everything in our lives are sharpened and ready. Our work then becomes a breeze. We are less frustrated. Things just seem to fall into place.

Each day of life you and I should strive for personal growth.

We should never reach the point in which we say, "I am sufficient; I am smart enough; I know what to do in any situation." Just as sure as we make these statements, a cool wind
blows and we're off course again or we forget to take care of
those things of importance like sharpening a blade. Worthy is
the man or woman who takes the time to prepare for any
situation ahead. Being prepared is half the battle. The second
half should prove to be a breeze! Good luck today with your
battles.

Giving Without Thought

"Give, and it shall be given unto you; good measure, pressed down, and shaken together, and running over, shall men give into your bosom. For with the same measure that ye mete withal it shall be measured to you again." --St. Luke 6:38

Renee and I were serving in our first appointment on a three-point charge (three churches which rotated Sundays and times of service). I was working full time with Juvenile Court Services and Renee attended college. I took a class or two at night at our local college as well, but found it very difficult to juggle everything. On Saturday and Sunday afternoons Renee and I would visit church members and catch-up on our reading assignments for classes. We made very little money in those first few years of marriage, but one thing we never forgot to do was pay our church tithes of 10% or more. On top of that, we were always wanting to give to different causes, especially to some of the kids I had on probation who came from very poor families.

I specifically remember one of those first few months awaiting our college grants to arrive when we completely ran out of money except for one twenty-dollar bill. On the way to church that Sunday, Renee and I decided to put it into the offering plate since we couldn't turn it into $200 by the next week. We did it in faith knowing it was our responsibility.

Some of you would say that we were stupid in doing so, but we felt relieved to get that $20 bill out of our hands and into the hands of God. We would eat light, we decided for the next two weeks, and pray that God would provide.

Sure enough, without any notice, a check arrived the very next day in the mail. I opened the envelope and a particular church member had sent us a check for $300! The note said that God had told her to send us the check without question. Can you believe that? What a mighty God we serve; one who knows our every need and responds when His children are struggling.

Since that first year of marriage, Renee and I have always given above-and-beyond our tithe to various causes, as well as to our churches served. We have never been in that position since over the last thirty-eight years. We give generously and often so that God can respond as needed with others who may be struggling. "Give and it shall be given unto you," may sound like payback, but we have never viewed it in that sense. We view it as being faithful first to God and then to our fellow man, never expecting anything in return. We know that our God is sufficient and would help us again should the need arise.

We have never been behind on any payments since that first year! The money we have needed has always been there. God has provided everything for us and oftentimes bountifully! To Him we give our praise, glory and honor. We must also recognize others who listen to God and respond as did that precious church member years ago.   When that wee-small voice calls, we should be ready and willing to answer. He (God) speaks to us in various ways! Listen and hear.

Inquisitive Ben

Our grandson, Benjamin, is wise beyond his five-years and is constantly amazing us with some neat insights. For instance, he and his mom passed a cemetery recently and Ben (as we call him) wanted to know why there were flowers on the graves. His mom told him that people put flowers there to honor the dead. Benjamin responded, "Why? They can't see them!"

On yet another occasion, Ben was having lunch with Renee and me and would not eat his beans. Renee ("Granny") told him that God would not be happy with him if he didn't eat his peas. Ben asked if he could use Granny's cell phone to call God and ask Him if he had to eat the beans. Granny replied, "Honey, you can't reach God on my cell phone," to which Ben replied, "Well, then you need to get a new phone!" Out of the mouth of babes!

Still yet on another occasion, he was helping his granny take dishes from the dishwasher to put them away when he noticed a large serving spoon with holes in it. He noticed those holes and wanted to know what happened to it because it wasn't like the other spoons. He thought that someone had ruined that spoon by putting holes in it.

When we are trying to explain Christ and salvation to people, we must remember to share in a straight-forward and simple manner so as not to confuse people. Theological babble will never lead folks to the Savior but a sharing of your simple faith will. God bless you as you impart to others God's plan of salvation.

192 CHARLES E. CRAVEY

Cowboys and Indians

As a child I vividly remember playing the innocent game of "Cowboys and Indians" with my friends. We would divide into the two groups and the Cowboys would hunt down the Indians to destroy them since, it was assumed, the Indians were the bad guys. After having played the part of Indian a few times, I began to be more sympathetic to their side. We (Indians) were always the "hunted," although the land originally belonged to us. Cowboys were supposedly "the Good Guys," but now I wasn't for sure. TV shows had glorified Cowboys as those brave souls who risked everything to "tame" the Wild, Wild West.

When we study the history of America it's most difficult to accept the grand atrocities wrought against the native Indian population here, all in the name of "Freedom." Why does freedom always seem to come at the expense of others, especially since the Indian was here first? Who gave us the right to take away the lives of countless Indians, tribes and families for the sake of establishing a homeland for ourselves? Where is the righteousness and justice in all of that? When you think about it, we were no different than the Iraqis who attempted to take over the nation of Kuwait, are we?

All Indians were eventually pushed onto Reservations and given very few concessions. Again, this clearly shows our prowess and power over an innocent population of native Americans.

Our first pilgrims came to America under the guise of religious freedom from the heavy taxation and repressive English rule. We traded that to become the repressors of the American Indian, taking away all of their rights and privileges and ways of life. When does one atrocity make another one right? Our religious freedom came at a very terrible cost to the Indian.

I'm sorry if you do not agree with my take on how America came into existence, but it's true. It was simply not right for our forebears to do what they did to the American Indian. And I could continue with our celebration of THANKSGIVING in this line of thinking. Where do you think that would fit into this discussion?

Lasting Impressions

The first person to truly touch my heart and make a lasting impression was my fourth grade teacher, Mrs. Evelyn Harris. Up until that day, I had been looked upon by most kids in my school as somewhat of a second-class citizen because my family and I lived in a ramshackle old clapboarded house and had very little income. My clothes were all hand-me-downs and my shoes had been well-worn by my two older brothers and never fit well. My hair was unkempt and I could never seem to keep my shirt tail packed in! Most kids ignored me and kept themselves in little cliques. I had nothing to offer them from my world.

On this particular occasion, I got into trouble on the play-ground and as punishment, Mrs. Harris asked me to stay after class for an hour. At the end of my punishment, Mrs. Harris left her desk and came to the back of the room where I was seated and sat down next to me. Facing me with kind and caring eyes, she began to tell me how important I was and what a charming young man I was becoming. She talked about how I should never feel intimidated by the other children but instead should use my talents and gifts to their greatest benefit. She stated that if I did that then the other children would begin to take notice and recognize my abilities. She knew that I was smart and could do better than a "C" average in my classes if I would only study and work harder. She was willing to even stay after school two days each week in order to tutor me.

Someone finally believed in me and saw beyond my outer facade and into my heart. She treated me with dignity and respect. Because of Mrs. Harris, I began to work harder and to study at home each night in order to impress my tutor and not my classmates. Mrs. Harris began to call on me more often when she knew that I could answer pertinent questions in class. I went from a "C" average student that year to straight "A's" because of her help and concern for me. I would never again be the cowering little introvert from my past. Now I was somebody, someone who could make a difference, someone who could help change the world.

I have repaid Mrs. Harris' kindness many times through the years by tutoring many young people, serving as a Boy Scoutmaster for 26 years, working with Juvenile Court Services, youth groups, youth retreats, and a host of other avenues to enable youth to be everything they can be and more! Thank you, Mrs. Harris. I'm sure God has you working hard up there in Heaven where you definitely belong.

Can't Choose Your Memories

You can't choose your memories - they just happen, often when you least expect them to. I was on the back porch of my home at fifteen when a radio announcer came on and gave a news flash that the great soul-singer, Otis Redding, had just died in a plane crash. Otis recorded that great hit, "Sitting On The Dock of the Bay," and was a rising star in the music world. He was also from Macon, Georgia, and that endeared him to my heart because I love Macon and have relatives and dear friends still living there. In fact, I knew the neighborhood where Otis grew up and had a couple of friends who had lived near him.

That day my heart dropped at such sad and tragic news. The music world was also saddened over the loss of this very talented singer and performer. That moment, frozen in time, and that memory has remained with me for the past 44 years! Amazing, isn't it? Other events have come and gone since then, but the vivid memory of that moment remains alive forever.

One may try to create lasting memories but there are no assurances that they will remain long after the moment has passed. Most lasting memories just happen - the death of a loved one, graduation, a traumatic event, the birth of a child, a serious surgery, etc. I vaguely remember our dating routines of four years, but I will never forget the day Renee and I were married! It is so crystal clear in my memory bank.

Remember, you can choose your friends, but you can't choose your memories. They just happen. Make the most of your memories and your life.

For Additional Copies:

IN HIS STEPS PUBLISHING
6500 Clito Road
Statesboro, Georgia 30461

Please enclose $14.95 per book
plus $5.00 for shipping.

www.ingramcontent.com/pod-product-compliance
Lightning Source LLC
LaVergne TN
LVHW051517080426
835509LV00017B/2093